SIS Volume XV, Number 3

Creating the Post-Communist Order

Post-Communist Politics
Democratic Prospects in Russia and Eastern Europe

by Michael McFaul

foreword by Stephen Sestanovich

The Center for Strategic
and International Studies
Washington, D.C.

Library of Congress Cataloging-in-Publication Data

McFaul, Michael, 1963-
    Post-communist politics / by Michael McFaul ; foreword by Stephen
Sestanovich.
        p. cm. — (Creating the post-communist order) (Significant issues
series, ISSN 0736-7136 ; v. 15, no. 3)
    Includes bibliographical references.
    ISBN 0-89206-208-8
    1. Political parties—Russia (Federation) 2. Political parties—Europe,
Eastern. 3. Post-communism—Russia (Federation) 4. Post-communism—
Europe, Eastern. 5. Democracy—Russia (Federation) 6. Democracy—Europe,
Eastern. I. Title. II. Series.
JN6699.A795M34 1993
324.247'009'049—dc20   93-7396
                                                                CIP

Cover design by Hasten Design Studio, Inc.

Contents

About the Author

Michael McFaul is a research associate at Stanford University's Center for International Security and Arms Control where he codirects a project on military conversion and privatization in the former Soviet Union. A former Rhodes scholar, he is also a research fellow at the Hoover Institution and a consultant for the National Democratic Institute for International Affairs. He has worked as a consultant for the "MacNeil/Lehrer Newshour" on PBS and as an International Research and Exchanges Board (IREX) researcher and lecturer at Moscow State University. He is the author with Sergei Markov of *The Troubled Birth of Russian Democracy* as well as articles in the Journal of Democracy, International Organization, and *International Security* on Russian politics and international relations.

Foreword

The story of the fall of communism and its replacement by a pluralist order can be told with children's-book simplicity. Once there was one of everything: one party, one television network, one news agency, one writers' union, one airline, one tourist bureaucracy, one manufacturer of cigarette filters. Then, as the very term *pluralism* suggests, one-of-everything began to give way to many-of-everything. The collapse of the old order was marked by a wild profusion of new institutions: newspapers and magazines, trade unions, commercial banks, commodity exchanges, professional schools, mystical sects, and so on. Not only is there now more than one writers' union in Moscow, there is also more than one Communist Party—and even more than one KGB.

The process of multiplication has been visible at every level. Czechoslovakia has become 2 countries; the Soviet Union, 15; in the case of Yugoslavia, the count is still under way. And it is not only the institutions of the old order that have disintegrated. With fragmentation taking place in every sector of society, the splintering of the democratic opposition movements that brought down communism was also inevitable. Solidarity, Civic Forum, Democratic Russia—almost all of the broad anti-Communist umbrella groups have yielded to new parties, movements, and other political organizations of the most extreme diversity. Had they not done so, it would be hard to say with conviction that they had created a truly pluralist order.

Westerners approach the emergence of post-Communist society with a mixture of confidence and incomprehension. Many parts of the process are bound to follow patterns with which we are relatively familiar. If the subject is de-monopolization of cigarette filter manufacturing, for example, there is little uncertainty about the ultimate goal nor fear that matters can go terribly awry. If too many new factories spring up, the worst that is likely to happen is that some will have to close down. Resources will be wasted and those who are involved in the new ventures may have to find a new livelihood, but apart from these costs the social impact of any "mistakes" is clearly bearable. In due course, supply and demand will come into balance. Once they do, post-Communist manufacturing—of cigarette filters or anything else—is unlikely to be very different from any other kind.

In politics, by contrast, uncertainty about the process of creating new institutions—and about the end result—is far greater. Success depends on cooperation among a much larger group of actors, the mechanisms of self-correction are much weaker, and mistakes can be much more lasting. In light of the extreme centralization of the ancien régime, the political fragmentation that has followed the revolution is both necessary and desirable, but it can also make coherent government impossible. Without parliamentary majorities able to deal with the difficulties of post-Communist society, popular dissatisfaction with the democratic experiment itself may quickly grow. It is such political disarray that makes the economic transition from central planning to a market especially hard to manage.

In *Post-Communist Politics*, Michael McFaul examines the chaotic new political systems that have emerged since the revolutions of 1989 brought down Communist governments across Eastern Europe. His assessment of the prospects for continued democratic consolidation in this region represents an important antidote to the pessimism that has often pervaded Western analysis. In particular, he shows that there is not just one route beyond the political monopoly of the Communist Party. Poland, Hungary, and Czechoslovakia had very different prerevolutionary political environments, very different revolutions, and now have quite different political party systems. None of these countries has been able to avoid recurrent political crises; each crisis has, in fact, been viewed routinely as proof that the entire post-Communist enterprise was collapsing at last. And yet all the new democracies have survived (even if Czechoslovakia did not survive as a country).

Political developments in Eastern Europe since 1989 suggest the sturdiness of post-Communist democracy, but they hardly prove that democracy will succeed everywhere. The largest question mark is, of course, Russia. Dr. McFaul provides evidence for both hopeful and despairing readings of Russia's likely future. The most negative indicator is this: In contrast to the new political systems of Eastern Europe, Russia still has no party system to speak of. As a consequence, it is still experiencing the politics of fragmentation; no governing majority has emerged. It is in part because of this fragmentation that many Russians believe their country needs a strong presidential system, but the Russian presidency is not yet such an office. Boris Yeltsin's power initially had a charismatic rather than an institutional basis and as such has been more easily challenged as the afterglow of the revolution begins to fade.

In these institutional terms, Russia has made the least progress of the countries examined in this book. Yet Dr. McFaul's argument, by assigning such importance to institutions, has its hopeful side: The record of Eastern Europe suggests that the holding of elections is the decisive spur to party development. By putting early elections on Russia's political agenda, both Boris Yeltsin and his opponents have identified the mechanism by which to regain the ground that has been lost since the coup of August 1991. Nothing is likely to help Russian democracy as much as early elections; by the same token, nothing could be more damaging than their cancellation.

Michael McFaul's careful comparative study of the new politics of Russia and Eastern Europe is the fourth and final book in a series published by the CSIS Russian and Eurasian studies program under the general rubric *Creating the Post-Communist Order*. The aim of the series has been to identify general conclusions that will help both participants and observers to understand better the revolution that is still unfolding around us.

We gratefully acknowledge the strong support we have received for this and other projects from the Lynde and Harry Bradley Foundation of Milwaukee.

Stephen Sestanovich
Director of Russian and Eurasian Studies, CSIS
April 1993

Acknowledgments

The author would like to thank Renee de Nevers, Larry Diamond, Lynn Eden, Joshua Freeman, David Holloway, Sergei Markov, Sarah Mendelson, Gregory Minjack, Donna Norton, Tova Perlmutter, Lazlo Poti, and Steve Sestanovich for comments on early drafts of this essay. Many of the ideas for this book were generated while the author was a Department of State Title VIII Fellow at the Hoover Institution and a Field Program Officer in Moscow for the National Democratic Institute for International Affairs. The views expressed here, however, do not reflect the official position of either of these institutions.

Introduction

Few events in the history of the modern world rival the revolutionary changes that erupted in Eastern Europe in 1989 and culminated in the breakdown of Soviet communism in August 1991. In two short years, the entire Soviet bloc collapsed, permanently recasting the international balance of power and the domestic politics of all the countries of the former Warsaw Pact and former Soviet Union.

With amazing uniformity, each new government emerging from Communist rule has aspired to reconstruct both state and society according to an identical set of ideas and institutions. Democracy is the ordering political principle, and capitalism is the coveted economic system.

Has the collapse of communism in Eastern Europe and the former Soviet Union ushered in a new era of liberal capitalism? Or will the East European transitions have other outcomes? Do different kinds of transitions lead to different kinds of democracies? No study can answer these questions conclusively, for the post-Communist transition in Eastern Europe and the former Soviet Union has only just begun. Nevertheless, a comparison of the political evolution of Poland, Hungary, Czechoslovakia, and Russia to date suggests important provisional conclusions. Such a comparison can help identify the factors that influence the transition from totalitarian rule, the forces that affected the emergence of democratic politics, and the relationship between these two sets of variables.

The Nature of Revolutionary Transitions

The transitions in Eastern Europe and the former Soviet Union are true revolutions, comparable to other great historical turning points. They involve "a sweeping, fundamental change in political organization, social structure, economic property control and the predominant myth of social order, thus indicating a major break in the continuity of development."[1] None of the countries of Eastern Europe or the former Soviet Union has completed this simultaneous change in the polity and economy, but most new leaders in the former Communist world strive to achieve such a revolutionary outcome.[2]

The difficulties of post-Communist transitions are more acute in many ways than those of democratic transitions in capitalist countries. Unlike recent democratizations in Latin America or Southern Europe, "soft-liners" in the ancien régimes of Eastern Europe and the former Soviet Union did not always initiate liberalization, nor did they seek to negotiate agreement between the old ruling classes and the new challengers.[3] In Hungary and the Soviet Union, reformers in the Communist Party indeed began the process of liberalization from above, while pacts between the Communist regime and democratic challengers initially regulated the pace and process of change in Poland and Hungary. In none of these anti-Communist revolutions, however, did strategies initiated by the Communist Party or bargains cut during the transition protect the property rights of the old rulers or define the parameters of the new polity.

The relationship between state and society is also a source of difficulty in post-Communist revolutions. Civil society is often "resurrected" in democratic transitions in capitalist countries, but in post-Communist transitions it must be created almost from nothing. Independent associations had formed in Poland and Hungary and had begun to develop in Czechoslovakia and the Soviet Union. These nascent civil societies erected within Communist systems did not, however, produce the kinds of social organizations and civic units necessary to support a democratic polity in a capitalist economic system.

Nonrevolutionary transitions can be mapped along known paths. True revolutions demand a blind leap from the old order to something new, with few institutional trusses or historical braces to guide the jump. The more change in socioeconomic structure and state institutions needed to create a capitalist democracy, the wider the gap between the old order and the new consolidated democracy.[4]

The size of these gaps has varied throughout East Central Europe and Russia. In Hungary, Janos Kadar's relatively liberal regime opened up space for independent economic and political activity, allowing a "second society" to develop outside the state. This cordial relationship between the state and society established a propitious context for an evolutionary transition from authoritarian to democratic rule. The combination of Hungary's liberal political and socioeconomic system under communism and the evolutionary transition from authoritarian rule, in turn, lessened the degree of revolutionary change necessary for the construction of a post-Communist democratic polity and capitalist economy.

The stages of transition in Poland and Czechoslovakia (and later the Czech Republic and Slovakia) were not so orderly. Neither regime promoted political or economic liberalization until right before its collapse, creating polarized situations in both states. At the outset, Poland's transition was less tumultuous, based on "roundtable" talks and then catalyzed by elections, while Czechoslovakia's revolution was decided in the streets. Once Communist rule collapsed, this relationship was reversed: Poland's socioeconomic transformation has required more revolutionary action than the attainment of similar objectives in the Czech Republic.

Russia's move from authoritarian rule to democratic governance has been, and will remain, the roughest and most revolutionary. Of all the countries considered here, Russia started reform with the most entrenched state-run command economy and also with little or no historical experience with capitalism or democracy. Although initiated from above by Mikhail Gorbachev, Russia's transition to democracy became extremely polarized, culminating in the collapse of one system and the birth of another.

The collapse of the one side in this polarized transition was not total, however, as the new Russian state did not seize the opportunity to dismantle Soviet institutions and organizations after the coup attempt in August 1991. These holdovers from the Soviet ancien régime, be it the system of soviets or even the Communist Party, began to reassert themselves once the initial euphoria of the "democratic" victory in August 1991 eroded. Unlike similar legacies from the Communist past in East Central Europe, these structures in Russia are still deeply entrenched. Consequently, the task of constructing a new democratic polity in Russia while at the same time promoting transformation of the economic system (and overseeing the collapse of an empire) is qualitatively greater than in any East Central European country.

This striking contrast between East Central Europe and Russia underscores both the likelihood of success for democracy in the former and the fragility of its prospects in the latter.

The Mechanics of Transition

New political leaders are not simply prisoners of history. Critical strategic decisions can enhance, or harm, the consolidation of a democratic polity. In all post-Communist states the timing, sequence, and rules of elections have determined whether political parties coalesce and establish stable intermediaries between the state and society.[5] Elections held before the total collapse of the Communist system tend to polarize political forces into two camps: Communist and anti-Communist. These situations are highly volatile and do not establish the social or institutional basis for a stable democracy. Once the Communist system folds, however, the sooner new elections are conducted—the sooner a "founding" election is held—the better the chances for the emergence of consolidated political parties upon which a stable democratic polity can be grounded.[6]

The countries in this study handled this problem in very different ways. Hungary convened the first and most successful founding election, in which political parties, not social movements or charismatic individuals, defined the menu of choices for voters. The timing of this election, held right after the collapse of communism but well before the beginning of economic reform, facilitated the development of political parties as the intermediaries between state and society. Hungary's electoral law also discouraged fringe parties and encouraged cooperation between like-minded individuals and social groups. Consolidated political parties, proportional representation, and the relatively smooth process of economic transformation have diminished the need for a strong executive.

Poland was the first Communist country to hold elections but the last to have a free and fair election based on political parties. The first Polish vote for a limited number of parliamentary seats armed Solidarity with a mandate for change but did not stimulate the formation of post-Communist political parties. The vote produced a polarized parliament that did not represent Polish society and could not govern effectively. This condition gave impetus for

Poland's second election, a vote to create a presidency and a referendum on Lech Walesa. Walesa's victory affirmed his personal
authority and established a presidential political system but did
little to consolidate political parties. Poland's third election was
the first in which the ballot was controlled by political parties. By
the time of this election, however, both major political parties to
emerge from Solidarity were associated with and blamed for the
severe hardship caused by economic reform, providing political
ammunition for new opposition parties. Low thresholds in
Poland's electoral law also provided opportunities for small parties to gain parliamentary seats. As a result, Poland's founding
election produced a weak and factionalized parliament.

The collapse of communism in Czechoslovakia was confrontational, chaotic, and sudden. The timing and sequence of Czech
and Slovak elections, however, helped shape smooth transitions in
each republic. Because founding elections were held after the
Communist collapse, neither parliament has been paralyzed by
struggles over fundamental issues.[7] Parties, not personalities or
movements, also assumed center stage in these founding elections, even if these parties had poorly defined social bases.
Electoral laws emphasizing proportional representation and promoting multiparty systems (not two-party systems) have impeded
the development of strong presidential offices in both republics.
The sequence of elections also fostered the peaceful split between
the Czech Republic and Slovakia.

The timing and sequence of elections in Russia as it began to
make the transition from communism were worse than in all the
other countries considered here. Russia's first election, in March
1990, produced a parliament polarized between "democrats" and
"Communists." Political parties had only begun to appear and did
not play any role in this election.[8] As in Poland, paralysis of parliament prompted a campaign to create a presidency. Elections for
this new office in June 1991, however, were not based on parties.
Rather, Boris Yeltsin, supported by the democrats, ran against
everyone else.

Since the collapse of communism, Russia has not held a major
election. Parties with new social bases have not developed, while
Russia's parliament has remained fractured and polarized, unable
to decide basic questions about a new political order. Because

economic reform has been particularly harsh in Russia, the current government is reluctant to call elections for fear of backlash. This situation has resulted in a very volatile transition in which democratic institutions such as regular elections or political parties have yet to play a role. As finally recognized by Russian leaders during the March 1993 crisis in government, convoking a founding election is necessary, although not sufficient, if Russia's transition to democracy is to continue.[9]

The timing and sequence of elections do not by themselves settle the course of post-Communist transitions. Historical legacies, ethnicity, even geography, remain crucial. The reform process in Poland, for instance, is eased by the extraordinary degree of national, cultural, and religious unity and the lack of disputes about borders or ethnic minorities.[10] Prospects for Russian democracy, at the other extreme, are threatened by secessionist minority movements within Russia and poorly defined borders between Russia and the other new nations of the former Soviet Union.

Geography also plays a role in democratization. Because of their location, Hungary and the Czech Republic experience the pull of the democratic West with much greater intensity than does Russia (let alone Uzbekistan or Tajikistan). By the same token, a democratic political system has become a precondition for "joining" the West, but some countries are more willing to pay the admission fee than others. Few Poles would doubt that Poland is in the heart of Europe. Whether Russia is in the West, in the East, or somewhere else is an ancient, yet ongoing, debate.

East Central Europe versus Russia

Democratic consolidation has proceeded much more rapidly in East Central Europe than in Russia. Polities in East Central Europe have evolved along different trajectories, among them both the creation (the Polish presidency) and dissolution (the Czechoslovak federation) of government institutions. Despite tremendous obstacles, all of these transitions from authoritarian rule in East Central Europe appear to be moving toward greater consolidation of democratic governments.

Russia's path is more ambiguous. The scale of revolutionary transformation required to create a capitalist democracy in Russia dwarfs all others. Russia's democratic project is complicated by thorny issues of state borders, secessionist movements, and poorly sequenced elections. Democracy is not preordained to fail, but the obstacles to consolidating democracy are much greater in Russia than in East Central Europe.

The heart of this study is the comparative context for the Russian transition, which is laid out in chapters 1 and 2. Chapter 3 discusses the origins and development of that transition, culminating with the August 1991 coup attempt. Chapter 4 analyzes the formation and consolidation of Russia's post-Soviet state, focusing on territorial integrity and the division of power among the executive, legislative, and judicial branches of government and among its different levels. Chapter 5 evaluates the reconstitution of Russian social movements, political parties, and civil society since the August coup. Chapter 6 concludes with a comparison of transitions from Communist rule to democratic governance in East Central Europe and Russia.

1
Transitions to Democracy in East Central Europe

Starting Points: The Nature of the Ancien Régime

Poland

Poland, Czechoslovakia, and Hungary each started the transition process with a very different historical legacy. Poland began the transition to democracy with a long and developed history of opposition to communism. The Polish People's Republic imposed after World War II never acquired toleration, let alone legitimacy, from Polish society, except for the brief splash of nationalist defiance by the Communist leaders in 1956. Given this intense antagonism between the party-state and the rest of society, social movements, whether worker protests in 1956, 1970, and 1976 or student revolts in 1968, always confronted the state rather than seeking to work with or within the state. By the late 1970s and beginning especially with the creation of Solidarity in 1980, Polish independent associations even sought to distinguish between what is the state's and what is (or should be) located in civil society. In making these distinctions precisely, always with special reference to Poland's "geopolitical realities," Poland's opposition forces aspired to carve a social and economic space for society not simply independent from the state, but totally unconnected with and oblivious to the state's existence. Eventually, however, Solidarity's "self-limiting revolution" collided with the state. If Soviet military intervention was to be avoided, the Polish state could not allow one-quarter of the population to be organized into overt opposition to the Communist regime.

    The imposition of martial law further exacerbated the state-society divorce in Poland, but it also destroyed the Communist Party's control of the state forever.[1] Under General Wojciech

Jaruzelski, the Polish military replaced the Polish United Workers' Party (PUWP) as Poland's governing organization until power was renegotiated with Solidarity. In contrast to all other countries in Eastern Europe or the Soviet Union, the collapse of the PUWP began years before the opening of the first roundtable talks, let alone before the first elections. In 1986, the PUWP claimed 2 million members; by March 1990, total membership had dropped to less than 67,000.[2] In January 1990, as a last attempt at salvaging a future, the PUWP changed its name to the Party of Social Democracy.

The decline of the Communist Party's monopoly of governance and the further delegitimization of the Polish military state were accompanied by an even greater commitment by Solidarity leaders (many of whom were in and out of jail at the time) to demarcating the border between the state and "private society." Throughout the decade of economic stagnation and political decay following martial law, Polish citizens still consciously created the most independent and vibrant civil society in Eastern Europe. Often overlooked, Poland's peasant population, the economic activity it generated, and the thriving Polish black market must also be considered as aspects of Polish civil society that existed under Communist rule. Furthermore, the Catholic church, an island of nonstate associational activity throughout Communist rule in Poland (and other periods of foreign occupation), served as a haven for the more overtly anti-Communist political activities, while more subtle forms of cultural and social protest such as the "Orange Alternative" helped to fill the void left after Solidarity's suppression. More generally, as Christine Sadowski has written,

> In fact, throughout the four decades of communism, Poles
> had more per capita voluntary associations and member-
> ships than any other East European country. The seeds of
> a civil society have been in place all along in small com-
> munities across Poland in a form that few observers
> noticed, especially when so many other sensational events
> were taking place in the country over the decades of
> Communist rule.[3]

The combination of a strong civil society (albeit at times suppressed and always bounded), an illegitimate Communist Party only partially involved in governance, and a military regime with reformist proclivities led many to believe that Poland would make the transition from authoritarian rule faster and more successfully than any other East European country. Not surprisingly, Poland was first out of the blocks in the transition from authoritarian rule.

Hungary

The path by which Hungary arrived at the moment of transition from authoritarian rule was very different from Poland's. Kadar's compromise with Moscow and the Hungarian people, after Hungary's bitter experience with political mobilization in 1956, forfeited political autonomy for economic maneuverability. In promising Moscow strict adherence to Warsaw Pact orthodoxy, Kadar gained freedom to pursue radical economic reforms that resulted in the introduction of the New Economic Mechanism in 1968. In asking the Hungarian people for passive acceptance rather than active support (or forced mobilization), Kadar promised them economic opportunity and a private life.[4] Kadar's "goulash communism" created space for and even promoted independent economic activities to coexist with the state economy.

Eventually, the development of this legalized "second economy" encouraged the evolution of a "second society" as well, independent of the state-party apparatus but devoid of political content.[5] Although by no means an open arena for independent association or a force exerting influence over the state, Hungarian society did attain a level of autonomy from the state rivaled only by Poland in the Eastern bloc. Hungarians did not consciously seek to create a civil society as an alternative to the Communist state, as was the case in Poland, but they did cultivate a type of "a-civil" society, that is, a society apolitical concerning opposition to the state but also neutral regarding subservience or obedience to it. In contrast to traditional conceptions of civil society, an "a-civil" society might be defined as one in which a great many activities take place outside the state, but with no direct connection, indirect leverage, or even desire for connection with or influence over the state. This peculiar condition of state-society relations set the stage for a peaceful and orderly transition from authoritarian rule.[6]

Czechoslovakia

Like Hungary's experience in 1956, the defining event in Czechoslovakia's pretransition Communist history was the crushing of the Prague Spring in 1968. Because the leadership of the local Communist Party had spearheaded liberalization from above, the counterrevolutionary regime installed by the Soviet Red Army in 1968 was decisively antireformist, oppressive, and orthodox. In sharp contrast to Kadar's 1956 compromise, the new Czechoslovakian Communist regime suppressed almost all associational activity not sponsored by the state or party, pushing any manifestation of "civil society" into the kitchen or onto the park bench. More than any other state in the region, Czechoslovakia most resembled (and aspired to be) a totalitarian system.

Like dissident activity in the Soviet Union, anti-Communist political activity in Czechoslovakia was channeled into moral protests carried out in isolation by individuals. As expressed by Czechoslovakia's greatest dissident, Vaclav Havel, the individual could find freedom within oneself, a location where the state could not seize it no matter what the external conditions of state terror or imprisonment. This moral crusade for individual humanity spawned the Charter 77 group, a coalition of dissidents who sought to secure protection from the state by linking their cause to transnational organizations—first and foremost to the Conference on Security and Cooperation in Europe (CSCE)—devoted to defending universal human rights. Charter 77 represented a moral protest, consciously nonideological and all-inclusive. Like their counterparts in Poland, this small band of dissidents sought to construct a parallel polis or "second culture" beyond the purview of state control.[7] Unlike Solidarity, however, Charter 77 lacked both organizational structures (for fear of repression) and concrete political demands on the state. The absence of reformers within the Czechoslovak government not only precluded dialogue between the state and its opponents but actively maintained a repressive police state atmosphere deleterious to any independent association.

The Transition Process

By the 1980s, all East European opposition movements had come to view direct political struggle—and especially violent confrontation—with their respective Communist regimes as unproductive. Instead, they sought to create civil societies not in direct competition with, but also not controlled by, the Communist state. Gorbachev, however, radically altered the limits of acceptable political conflict. His new political thinking about foreign policy encouraged soft-liners within East European Communist Parties to experiment with political and economic reforms and censured hard-liners resisting change. At the same time, Soviet foreign policy makers gradually removed the specter of military intervention as a viable policy option, no matter how far reforms proceeded or to what extent opposition amassed itself. This new "geopolitical reality" sparked a sequence of challenges to Communist rule throughout the Eastern bloc. Despite a common precipitator, change was not uniform. Rather, the mode of transition in each East European country was shaped by the historical characteristics of its state-society relations during the Communist era.

Poland's Pact Unraveled

Unable to revive the PUWP or legitimate his government, Jaruzelski finally attempted significant political reforms from above. Beginning with the amnesty for political prisoners and the formation of an advisory board of Solidarity activists and church leaders in 1986, Jaruzelski sought to attain at least a modicum of political acceptance in order to execute a vitally needed economic austerity program. The following year, Jaruzelski tested his strategy by holding a referendum on his economic program. The gambit failed miserably, forcing Jaruzelski to attempt even more radical political compromises with the opposition. As strikes erupted again in 1988, Jaruzelski's government came to the sobering conclusion that only some form of compromise with Solidarity could move Poland out of its debilitating stalemate.[8] Soon thereafter, the roundtable began.

The Solidarity that assumed the opposite side of the table in these negotiations with the government did not have the same internal cohesiveness or external support it had enjoyed in 1981. Although almost all the senior figures and factions from 1980–1981 came together again in 1988, the Solidarity coalition was a collection of heterogenous ideological groups and ideas, temporarily allied behind the symbol of Solidarity's past.[9] Nor did

Solidarity have an unequivocal mandate from society to negotiate on its behalf because the Polish population was neither mobilized nor optimistic about the first sessions of the roundtable talks. According to Solidarity leader Karol Modzelewski, "This mass activism [of 1980–1981] played virtually no role in 1988 and none at all during the round-table negotiations in 1989."[10] Polls confirmed Modzelewski's observation. By 1985, only 22 percent of those polled identified themselves as former Solidarity members. In March 1989, only 30 percent of those polled wanted to join the now-legal Solidarity movement, while 47 percent stated that they had no intention of joining.[11]

This kind of power balance between a weak but still entrenched state and a quickly reconstituted opposition with an uncertain mandate, all in the context of still fluid geopolitical realities, created propitious conditions for a pact between the reformist wing in the government and compromisers within the opposition. Significantly, and in sharp contrast to attempts in Russia at concluding pacts, the reformer Jerzy Rakowski negotiated on behalf of the government, while Solidarity radicals like Andrzejy Gwiazda, Marian Jurczyk, and the Orange Alternative, who resisted negotiations with the government, were pushed to the side by more conciliatory leaders within Solidarity. As observed in other transitions, pacts reflect an interdependency between the opposing forces in that neither side can achieve its desired objectives without the other. The Polish ancien régime looked to a pact as a way to stave off total collapse.[12] The opposition saw negotiations as a means to make incremental steps toward further political participation.[13]

The roundtable agreement, announced in April 1989, gave the opposition the opportunity to compete for government positions through elections, scheduled for June 1989. In a move typical of a negotiated pact (as opposed to a revolutionary takeover), however, the ruling government allowed only segments of the government to be open to contest, a limitation that the radical wing of Solidarity rejected. Members of the newly created upper parliamentary chamber, the Senate, were elected through open elections, but 65 percent of the seats of the existing lower parliamentary chamber, the Sejm, were reserved for the PUWP and its allies, as was the presidency itself for the first six-year term. Through such a compromise, Jaruzelski's government hoped to gain popular legitimacy, at the same time capturing and perhaps even co-opting the opposition in an impotent parliamentary chamber. Given the historical context of the time (April 1989), Solidarity's leaders (and the rest of the world) nonetheless considered the pact a monumental step toward genuine democratic rule in Poland.

Retrospectively, the June 1989 elections revealed that Solidarity had underestimated its real leverage at the roundtable. Propelled by a successfully reconstructed united front for the election campaign, Solidarity captured 99 of the 100 seats in the newly created Senate and all 161 seats reserved for non-Communists in the Sejm. Although the remaining 299 seats (65 percent) were preassigned to the PUWP and its allies, only three Communist Party candidates managed to acquire more than 50 percent of the vote in uncontested races, while the majority of Communist candidates for these reserved seats won only 5 to 25 percent of the vote.[14]

Solidarity's tremendous election victory precipitated an immediate debate about the renegotiation of the roundtable pact, demonstrating the power of first elections as a method of mobilizing anti-Communist sentiment. After much haggling, the new parliament agreed to elect Jaruzelski as president in July 1989, but in return gained the Solidarity leader, Tadeusz Mazowiecki, as prime minister the following month, thereby creating the first non-Communist government in Eastern Europe in more than 40 years. Communists were given the ministries of defense and interior, but the rest of the new government was composed of Solidarity leaders and representatives of the Peasant Party and the Democratic Party, former allies of the PUWP that cut ties with the Communists after the election.

Hungary's Negotiated Transition

Given Hungary's unique historical compromise in 1956, the transition from authoritarian rule in this state resembled a reforma, not a ruptura, distinguishing the Hungarian mode of transition from the more revolutionary upheavals in Czechoslovakia, Russia, and even Poland.[15] The reform wing of the Hungarian Socialist Workers' Party (HSWP) initiated and actively supported liberalization.[16] Well before the dramatic events of 1989, several reformers within the HSWP realized that the Kadar compromise was eroding as the Hungarian economy began to slow.[17] These Communist reformers organized to take control of the party and the state after pushing Kadar aside in May 1988 and replacing him with Karoly Grosz. In February 1989, the HSWP relinquished its monopoly as the leading actor in Hungarian politics. In June 1989, the Hungarian regime further liberalized by creating a new four-person presidency consisting of Grosz and radical reformers Rezso Nyers, Imre Pozsgay, and Miklos Nemeth.

In contrast to Poland, Czechoslovakia, or even Russia, reform and reorganization within the Hungarian ancien régime, not revolutionary movements from below, pushed the pace of democratic transition.[18] The comparison with the Soviet case is especially striking. Whereas radical reformers within the Communist Party of the Soviet Union (CPSU) eventually had to quit (in July 1990 at the Twenty-eighth Party Congress) to push the pace of change against an intransigent leadership, the Hungarian reformers within the party managed to continue to push the pace from within. These reformers from above instituted many salient features of a democratic polity well before being ousted entirely, most important among them being a constitutional amendment passed in October 1989 that permitted and protected a multiparty democracy. Sensing the Communist Party's demise, the Hungarian National Assembly began to act as an independent political entity well before the first free elections were held, setting important precedents for the newly elected body in 1989.

The Hungarian opposition was virtually invented by the swift and radical actions of Imre Pozsgay's new regime. A handful of Hungarian dissident circles had organized in the late 1980s, including the group of intellectuals that published Beszelo, the Democratic Opposition that published the "Social Contract" (a treatise on the failure of Kadarism), and the Hungarian Democratic Forum, a collection of populist writers and local leaders that formed in 1987 in part because of prodding from the liberal wing of the HSWP.[19] None of these groups, however, espoused overtly anti-Communist doctrines or revolutionary strategies. Nor did they represent massive6 movements. As late as the fall of 1989, the Hungarian Democratic Forum, the largest non-

Communist organization in Hungary at the time, could boast only 20,000 members.[20]

The notion of a Hungarian roundtable, then, which lasted from June to September 1989, was inspired by reformers from within the Hungarian ruling regime and by the Polish experience. In contrast to Poland, however, 30 years of peaceful coexistence between the Hungarian party-state and society fostered a congenial atmosphere for negotiations. Whereas Solidarity leaders had to negotiate with their formers captors to begin Poland's transition, members of the Hungarian opposition were invited to a table at which half of their interlocutors were already prepared to relinquish dictatorial power.

Pozsgay and the reformers within the Hungarian Communist regime realized that the hard-liners of the party had to participate in the negotiations if the negotiations were to succeed. Success at this stage, however, did not mean the complete collapse of Communist rule in Hungary. These progressive Communists still hoped to retain power, but by democratic means. Pozsgay and his cohorts believed that if they moved quickly and were perceived as the instigators of democratic reforms, they would be able to win elections, especially if alternative parties were slow to organize.

Because none of the organizations at the roundtable had a popular mandate, negotiating were neither constrained nor guided by a recognized sense of the balance of forces within society. This ambiguity of power created fluidity and flexibility in the negotiation process. Moreover, because no one had a mandate, everyone had to be represented. The roundtable had to be expanded to include a third side comprising six social organizations and trade unions, while dozens of "experts" from all sides accompanied the official delegates to the negotiations.

Events in Poland dramatically strengthened the negotiating position of the opposition parties and movements. In the wake of the PUWP's election disaster in June 1989, the non-Communist Hungarian parties at the roundtable refused to accept any conditionality on elections. The ruling authorities eventually accepted these demands, not out of weakness, but because of a false sense of strength; they believed that they still had enough popular appeal to win a free election. In addition to removing any conditions on elections, the Hungarian opposition movements also negotiated a complex election law based on proportional representation with high thresholds for winning parliamentary seats.[21] This law, in conjunction with the successful referendum that postponed the appointment of the president until after parliamentary elections, helped to consolidate weak and unknown parties, while discriminating against fringe groups and individual leaders.

The Hungarian Communists preferred to hold presidential elections before parliamentary elections, believing that the electorate's familiarity with their candidate—Imre Pozsgay—would ensure his victory over the handful of unknown figures representing the democratic opposition. The fate of Hungarian Communists, reformist or otherwise, looked very different after the parliamentary elections. The parliament was constituted by proportional representation, which heavily favored parties over individuals. The new parliament, elected in the spring of 1990 with a clear anti-Communist mandate, chose a president based on the new constellation of power in the non-Communist parliament.

In a critical tactical error, the Hungarian Democratic Forum boycotted the referendum elections, fueling rumors that it was still affiliated with the HSWP. The error, however, may have been good for Hungarian democracy in the long run because it allowed the initiator of the referendum, the Alliance for Free Democrats, to gain tremendous exposure from the process, proving once again the importance of electoral processes for the development of political parties. After the elections, the Alliance successfully established a real, yet non-Communist, parliamentary opposition to the Forum.

Hungary's mode of transition, then, was determined as much by the timing and sequencing of the "founding election" as by the terms of the roundtable. Perhaps most important to the consolidation of democracy in Hungary, the first elections were deliberately postponed for several months by the democratic opposition until real political parties had formed. This delay both weakened the ruling government and strengthened the opposition parties. Given the paucity of political organization outside the party at the time, Pozsgay's party could have won elections in the spring or summer of 1989. The dramatic collapse of Communist regimes throughout the region during the fall of 1989, however, dramatically discredited all Communists, progressive or otherwise. The reform wing of the HSWP attempted to remake itself by renaming the party the Hungarian Socialist Party in October 1989, but only 50,000 of the 720,000 former Communist Party members rejoined. Conservative Communists retained the old name and formed their own party. Within months, Pozsgay and the other Communist reformers moved from being recognized as the first in a new line of political leaders to the last in a long line of Communist regimes.

Meanwhile, outside the Communist ranks, Hungary's new political parties had the time and opportunity to establish national reputations. During this period, all non-Communist parties had to validate their anti-Communist credentials, especially the Hungarian Democratic Forum, which had earlier supported the reformist wing of the HSWP. The dissolution of the HSWP several months *before* the first elections, however, removed the bipolar straitjacket of Communists versus anti-Communists from the election campaign. Whereas Solidarity in 1989 and Democratic Russia in 1990 had to unite opposition forces in anti-Communist fronts during the first free elections, the Hungarian "anti-Communist" forces were already arguing among themselves before their first experiment with democracy. The Hungarian Democratic Forum appealed to rural, nationalist constituencies while the Alliance for Free Democrats, the party manifestation of the Democratic Opposition, adopted a more urban, liberal profile. This electoral environment allowed parties to develop political programs and accompanying social bases not confined to simple anticommunism. Moreover, in the first elections conducted before the collapse of Communist state power, the ruling ancien régime ensured a role for itself in the newly elected government, whether through prearranged political pacts as in Poland or rigged election rules as in Russia. In Hungary, a coalition government of new political parties established the first new democratic government.

The context and conditions of Hungary's first free elections in the spring of 1990, then, were vastly different from Poland's first election. No seats were allocated to the Communists by a "pacted" transition. On the contrary, the HSWP and its Socialist Party outgrowth were in rapid retreat, especially after November 1989. Moreover, real political parties had existed long enough to develop alternative political platforms but not long enough to undergo the massive proliferation of parties typical after the collapse of united fronts.

This combination of factors for the "founding election" produced an auspicious basis for a Western-style Hungarian democracy. The Hungarian Democratic Forum won the largest number of seats in the parliament and was easily able to establish a majority government with two smaller parties of a similar ideological orientation.[22] The Alliance for Free Democrats, the second largest party in parliament, joined forces with the Federation of Young Democrats (FIDESZ) to establish a liberal opposition. Parties affiliated with the former HSWP won a significant minority but assumed no role in the formation of Hungary's new government.

Transition in Czechoslovakia

If Hungary's mode of transition represented quintessential *reforma*, Czechoslovakia's path from authoritarian rule epitomized *ruptura* in its most powerful form. Inspired first by fleeing East Germans, the renunciation of the Brezhnev Doctrine, and then the fall of the Berlin Wall, an officially sanctioned student demonstration on November 17, 1989, erupted into a massive anti-Communist protest that was brutally suppressed by the police. Allegedly, the demonstration was concocted by liberals within the Czechoslovak Communist Party as a cover for a "palace coup." The liberals hoped to cite the demonstration as justification for their seizure of control of the party; they would then negotiate a pact with Czechoslovakia's nascent political opposition movements. The following day, students joined forces with Czech cultural figures to demonstrate against police brutality, triggering the formation of Civic Forum in the Czech Republic on November 19 and Public Against Violence in Slovakia on November 20. Within a week, these two groups had issued their revolutionary programs, which included a demand for the end of the Communist monopoly control over politics and the creation of a multiparty democracy.[23]

Unlike the situations in Poland or Hungary, however, these new opposition movements could not enter into negotiations with the ancien régime because no genuine "soft-line" faction existed within the Czechoslovak Communist Party. Yet, even if desirable, the newly formed opposition movements had little authority to enter into any form of negotiation with the government that was not ratified by a plebiscite on the streets. The locus of power in this transition, unlike that of Poland or Hungary, was situated in the massive, daily demonstrations. Under these circumstances, a revolutionary transformation or a counterrevolutionary suppression was the only possible outcome.

On November 28, the day after a massive strike in which roughly 80 percent of the Czechoslovak work force participated, the hard-line regime resigned. The following day, the Federal Assembly amended the constitution to eliminate the "leading role" of the Communist Party. After conferring with Civic Forum, Prime Minister Ladislav Adamec formed a new government in December, in which 3 of 21 ministers were not Communists. This weak attempt at sharing power, however, did not reflect the new balance of power in the country as manifested in the streets. Empowered by their numbers and encouraged by the pace of change in neighboring states, the new Czechoslovak opposition would not tolerate a negotiated transition. Instead, the "Government of National Understanding," in which the majority of ministers were not Communists, was formed on December 10. Vaclav Havel replaced Gustav Husak as president on December 29, 1989. The entire "Velvet Revolution" took little more than a month. Pacts, roundtables, or even elections were not a part of the revolutionary transition. Instead, an entirely new set of political leaders peacefully seized control of the state without any obligations to the past order.

2
Democratic Polities in East Central Europe

Poland's Path to Democratic Consolidation

The balance of forces changed dramatically in Poland following the revolutions throughout the rest of Eastern Europe. Poland's pact between the opposition and the Communist regime was negotiated in the perceived shadow of a potential Soviet intervention. When that specter disappeared in the fall of 1989, Poland's ancien régime lost all political leverage. Yet, vestiges of Poland's pact still left traceable legacies in defining the path of transition from authoritarian rule and influenced the course of change toward democratic consolidation. Poland's peaceful and negotiated transition meant that the ancien régime was not crushed as in other revolutions. Subsequent governments had to navigate around old Communist structures, or occupy them, or let them gradually die. Solidarity did not assume control of the State Security Office until July 1990. Jaruzelski remained president until December 1990. The Polish military forces are still commanded by the same officers who implemented martial law in December 1981.

In addition, the sequence of elections and partial elections established by the terms of the roundtable inhibited consolidated party formation. Solidarity competed in the first Polish elections as a united, anti-Communist front rather than as a party with its own program or set of parties.[1] Unlike the first Hungarian voters, Poles did not vote in their first elections for a kind of anticommunism (let alone some positive program). In other words, the first Polish elections were not "founding elections" of a multiparty democracy but a means of undermining authoritarian rule.

First elections that pit social movements or united fronts against Communist incumbents neither establish coherent, representative governments nor create propitious preconditions for

14

new political parties to compete in a second round of elections. Polarized parliaments after semi-free elections can be more detrimental to progressive change than even governing bodies fully controlled by Communists. As discussed in detail below, this dictum was especially true regarding the situation in Russia after the March 1990 elections. These divided governments make the democrats look ineffective.

In Poland, even after Mazowiecki became prime minister, the Communists still controlled enough seats in the Sejm to block or at least delay new legislation, including new laws that would influence the future reconstruction of the Polish government. One of the most contentious issues before the new parliament in 1991 concerned the new election law. Despite proposals from President Lech Walesa to introduce high voter thresholds for parties seeking parliamentary representation, the law finally passed in June favored small parties and especially those with concentrated local support, ensuring that the newly constituted parliament would be divided among dozens of parties rather than a consolidated handful.[2] Ironically, because of these delays over the new electoral laws, Poland was the first East European state to embark upon political reform but the last to have a fully free and open election. Even Albania had free elections before Poland.

Poland's second election for the presidency, in December 1990, did not help the formation of a multiparty system either. Choices were not defined by parties or party programs fashioned in accordance with post-Communist Polish society. Already by the time of the elections, Mazowiecki was affiliated with Citizens' Movement—Democratic Action (ROAD), while Walesa was identified with (but not a member of) the Center Alliance. Stanislaw Timinski was not the candidate of any party; rather, his candidacy produced a party, the X party. As is typical of presidential elections, however, votes were cast for individuals, not parties. Just as Solidarity won the first election based on its past reputation, so Walesa ran and won as the hero of Poland's past anti-Communist struggle, not because of his program for Poland's future. Whereas most countries in transition from authoritarian rule have had one election based on the past, Poland had two.

Poland's third major round of elections—elections for parliament in October 1991—was the first in which choices were formed on the basis of parties.[3] During the presidential election, the "war at the top" within Solidarity precipitated the collapse of the movement (although not the trade union) and the initial formation of political parties.[4] The split coalesced around two central tendencies within the movement: the liberal intelligentsia versus the more nationalistic right-of-center grouping (an oversimplified characterization, but one that captures the essence of the divide). Prime Minister Mazowiecki headed the first faction by forming ROAD in July 1990.[5] Jaroslav Kaczynski, a former close associate of Walesa's, consolidated the other faction under the banner of the Center Alliance.[6] Timothy Garton Ash depicted the initial divisions between these two groups:

> The real issue, says Lech Walesa, is "pluralism" versus the "new monopoly" of his former advisers. No, it is parliamentary constitutionalism versus extraordinary populism, says Geremek. It is Europeans against nationalists, says Adam Michnik. No, say others, the real conflict is between underrepresented workers and overrepresented intelligentsia. Or between country and city. Or simply between those who now have power and those who want it: the Ins and the Outs. Then someone else comes along and says . . . that after all the fundamental argument is still between the Left and Right.[7]

Had these parties formed and competed in elections immediately after the fall of communism, they might have established the basis for a stable, biparty system in Poland. When they came to compete against each other, however, both were already affiliated with discredited new governments; both entered into the third election as incumbent parties at a time in the Polish transition when voters were enduring the brunt of painful economic reforms, while the menu of choices (i.e., parties) had yet to be narrowed by a "founding election."[8] On the contrary, Poland boasted almost 300 parties in 1991.[9]

The result was fragmentation. Twenty-nine parties won seats in parliament. The liberal Democratic Union—the coalition of leading Solidarity intellectuals such as Mazowiecki, Adam Michnik, and Jacek Kuron, received the largest single share of the vote, but that was only 12.3 percent, placing them just ahead of the Democratic Left Alliance, a coalition of former Communists, which received 12 percent.[10] No other party received more than 10 percent. This divided parliament produced and destroyed three coalition governments within one year.[11]

Executive-Legislative Reorganization

Since the beginning of Poland's transition, both the offices of president and prime minister have been occupied by different individuals. The balance of power between these two posts, and between the executive and legislative branches of government more generally, has changed over the course of the transition. As long as Jaruzelski remained president, few objected to the largely ceremonial status of the post. Walesa's candidacy and victory for the presidential post in December 1990, however, radically altered the debate about the de jure and de facto power of the executive office.

Noting that Poland's democracy suffers from the disease of immaturity, Walesa argued that a strong executive was necessary to lead the country through harsh but necessary economic reforms.[12] During his brief tenure as president, he repeatedly raised the specter of banning parliament and ruling by decree if the legislative body failed to stay the course of radical economic reform. When his first two candidates for prime minister were rejected by the newly elected parliament in December 1991, Walesa called on parliament to give him sole authority to appoint the government as well as special powers to rule by decree in extraordinary circumstances. The crisis of executive authority even aroused rumors of a military coup and a return to martial law. These ambiguities of governmental divide were resolved, at least temporarily, when the Polish state adopted the "small constitution" in 1992 as an interim step toward delimiting the powers of the parliament and the presidency.

Factors of Consolidation

Party proliferation in the parliament, coupled with power struggles between the executive and legislative branches of government, gives the appearance of a democracy in crisis—unconsolidated, immature, and on the verge of collapse. Juxtaposed to these

dangerous tendencies, however, are several major questions
already answered by Poland's new democracy. First and foremost,
Poles know what and where Poland is and what and where Poland
is not. Deciding this fundamental question of state boundaries is a
fundamental, first step toward consolidating a stable democracy.
As Dankwart Rustow observed,

> democracy is a system of rule by temporary majorities. In
> order that rulers and policies may freely change, the
> boundaries must endure, the composition of the citizenry
> be continuous.[13]

Because Poland is a true nation-state, the Polish polity is not
threatened by secessionist movements or expansionist inclina-
tions. Institutions such as the Catholic church add further glue to
Poland's territorial and political homogeneity.

In addition, because Poland was the first East European state
to embark upon political reform, this new polity has already has
navigated several transfers of power at the highest levels of government through a democratic process. Four prime ministers have
surrendered power peacefully to a successor, as well as one president. Given Walesa's alleged authoritarian proclivities, his replacement as president will be the real test of how consolidated these
procedures have become. Walesa, however, has neither espoused
an intention nor demonstrated a desire to forsake the democratic
process that placed him in power.

Procedural minimums for a functioning democracy have also
been guaranteed and protected as norms of the new Republic of
Poland, including universal suffrage, freedom of expression and
association, almost no restrictions regarding who can run for
elected office, and elections as a means for selecting government
officials.[14]

Moreover, the conscious commitment to the construction of a
civil society by the Polish opposition even before liberalization,
the enduring presence of the Catholic church, and the new explosion of free market activity combine to create a burgeoning civil
society. After martial law, Polish society never reverted to its pre-
1980 status but remained a civil society awaiting liberation.[15] As
Adam Michnik recalled, "Instead of resembling a Communist system after victorious pacification, this situation resembles a

democracy after a military *coup d'etat.*"[16] When Communist rule was rolled back, Poland witnessed an explosion of political and social activity outside of the state. Although Polish civil society will be reorganized according to the new conditions of postcommunism, this history of independent political organization will be an asset to democratic consolidation.

Poland has also acquired a significant degree of national consensus on the kind of government it wants and the basic principles of its economy. Despite factions within the parliament or battles of power between the president and the prime minister, no major political force in Poland has advocated the complete abandonment of democracy or the return to communism. If democracy was viewed before the fall of the Communist regime as an instrument for gaining power, democracy has now become a principle of state governance and organization.[17] Even Walesa's calls for rule by decree have been couched in temperate tones, with references to constitutional amendments and respect for the rule of law. Instead of simply calling out the military, Walesa is trying to secure greater executive power by amending the constitution.

Extreme Catholic and nationalist political organizations have challenged the democratic norm by advocating the creation of a "Catholic State of the Polish Nation." According to Adam Michnik, advocates for developing the former use "the language of democratic debate; the latter, the language of insinuation and hatred. For the former, the nation is a community of culture; for the latter, a community of blood."[18] The Catholic church's expanding direct participation in Polish politics does suggest that the separation of church and state (an idea now associated in Poland with communism) could diminish and thereby threaten minority rights, suppress alternative programs, and foster an "uncivil" society. Anti-Semitic incantations during the October 1991 elections in a country with less than a 1 percent Jewish population reflected this tendency. In recognizing these potentially dangerous trends, however, it is also important to note what has not happened. Human rights abuses have been minimal. Fascist parties are still not prominent. Even anti-Communist campaigns have been mild thus far.[19]

Regarding the economy, Poland has also achieved a level of consensus sometimes obscured by parliamentary struggles and vicious election campaigns. Although the process has only just begun, preliminary evaluations of the East European experiment with dismantling Communist economies suggest that the more radical the reform, the more severe the initial political backlash. Paradoxically, however, the more radical the first assault on economic reform, the more quickly a consensus can develop about the general direction of the economy. In Poland, several parties capitalized on the backlash against radical economic reform by criticizing the "shock therapy" plan of Leszek Balcerowicz during the October 1991 elections. The Center Alliance, for instance, coined the slogan "breakthrough" to symbolize a departure from recession, the elimination of wage controls, subsidies for agriculture, increased unemployment benefits, and improved social services. After taking office, however, Prime Minister Olszewski of the Center Alliance appointed a close associate of Balcerowicz as finance minister and vowed not to deviate significantly from Poland's shock therapy course.[20] Even the Democratic Left Alliance, the former Communists, realize that Poland must create a market, capitalist economy. Debate about the economy has not been polarized between communism or capitalism. Rather, political battles are fought over the kind of capitalism Poland should construct.

Furthermore, the muting of the former opposition has also advanced consensus. Curiously for a country with a long tradition of dissidents, the decline of neo-Communists and the absence of a resurgence of neonationalists have also been accompanied by the declining role of radical liberals in politics. Although the Democratic Union, the political body representing this voice, received the largest percentage of the vote in October 1991, the party could not find allies to form a coalition government and was closed out of all leadership positions in both the Sejm and Senate. As one of Poland's leading dissidents, Adam Michnik, lamented, "The time for people like myself to engage in politics has come to an end."[21]

Poland thus has attained a degree of consensus regarding the "rules of the game" for political competition and a minimum level of agreement regarding the basic principles or ultimate values of the Polish nation-state.[22] Of course, opposing factions and parties will continue to support different specific government policies, but their debates are contained within an ideological spectrum that does not threaten the basic organizing principles of the state or the economy. Consensus over ultimate values is highly desirable because it can greatly facilitate consolidation, but it is not a precondition to democracy. Agreement about the rules of game, however, is a precondition. Otherwise, political battles become unpredictable and not confined to democratic procedures. As for specific policies of a given government, those are the domain of democratic competition. Consensus on this third area may be more damaging than constructive in the successful consolidation of a democratic state.

Hungarian Consolidation

Hungary's carefully negotiated and sequenced transition from authoritarian rule has endowed the new democracy, at least in the short term, with several consolidating features. Because the Communist regime had collapsed and political parties had already formed, Hungary's "founding election" served to consolidate parties and their roles rather than disperse or dilute power. Two major parties, not one movement or a dozen equally small parties, emerged from the transition: the Hungarian Democratic Forum and the Alliance for Free Democrats.

The two major parties capitalized on existing economic and geographical cleavages to construct specific social bases well before new social structures emerged from capitalism. The Hungarian Democratic Forum appealed to the countryside with overtly nationalist rhetoric to establish a right-of-center party. This party has championed "national liberalism," a fusion of conservative, Christian, and nationalist attitudes toward social issues with a more cautious stance regarding economic reform. In striving to be the "union of people's national thought," the Forum has deliberately avoided developing a particular class base. The Alliance for Free Democrats turned to the urban intelligentsia for its bases of support. This party has promoted a rapid transformation of the economy coupled with a liberal social agenda. The other "liberal" party, the Federation of Young Democrats, supports a similar mix of economic and social policy but with a particular slant toward people under 35.

The success of the two major parties has fostered the functioning of a stable Hungarian parliament. Although substantive ideological cleavages divide these new parties, the parliament has maintained a sufficient degree of consensus to pass a tremendous quantity of new legislation during its short history. The Hungarian Democratic Forum and the Alliance of Free Democrats even signed a pact of mutual understanding whereby they agreed that the introduction of martial law, changes in defense policy, a law on referenda, and a variety of other leading issues should be decided in parliament by a two-thirds majority. In addition to this concession, the ruling Hungarian Democratic Forum also allowed the Alliance to nominate their own Arpad Goncz as Hungary's first post-Communist president. Finally, the representative balance between the two major parties is more pronounced than in any other new democracy in Eastern Europe in that the Hungarian Democratic Forum controls the national parliament but the Alliance enjoys a controlling majority in many local government councils.

The lack of political heroes in Hungary's transition has also fostered competition between the major political parties and balance between the executive and legislative branches of power. Hungary's transition from authoritarian rule had no Lech Walesa, Vaclav Havel, or Boris Yeltsin. Although single, charismatic leaders are extremely beneficial for opposition movements during polarized revolutionary situations, these same leaders can hinder the development of pluralistic competition during the period of consolidation. Despite Prime Minister Jozsef Antall's bid for more authoritarian power, neither he nor any other Hungarian leader commands sufficient support from the people to establish a populist dictatorship.

Institutions of Democratic Governance

As determined by the 1989 referendum, the Hungarian parliament, not the people, names the president, subordinating executive power to the legislative branch of government. The leaders of the Alliance for Free Democrats, the initiators of the referendum, wanted to avoid Hungary's previous experiment with democracy in which a strong executive—Regent Admiral Miklos Horthy— dominated a weak and split parliament. As in all other East European transitions, however, an acute debate has erupted over the division of power between the legislative and executive branches of government. Disputes over spheres of authority have focused on two issues: the division of power between the president and the prime minister and the division of power between the prime minister and the parliament.

The combination of the 1989 referendum and the constitutional amendments introduced immediately after the 1990 parliamentary elections severely restricted the power of the president. Unlike Poland, Czechoslovakia, or Russia, Hungary did not opt for a mixed parliamentary-presidential system but has instead adopted a parliamentary system. Hungary's new president, Arpad Goncz, has attempted to assert his authority as "head of state" on issues regarding foreign representation, command of the armed forces, and presidential appointments. Decisions over jurisdiction have been difficult and politically charged, but all have been decided by a democratic process and none has threatened the basic integrity of the new Hungarian state.

Similarly, moves by Prime Minister Antall to acquire more autonomous power have challenged the balance of power within the new democracy, but they have not denigrated the democratic process. Antall's authoritarian proclivities have alienated many within the parliament that elected him, forced the resignation of several key figures from his own party, the Hungarian Democratic Forum, and precipitated a split within one of the parties in his coalition. As Peter Tolgyessi, chairman of the Alliance of Free Democrats, explained,

> I always maintained that Hungary needed legitimate government with adequate powers. So the consolidation of our Prime Minister's authority ought to be regarded as a positive development. But the government set up by the Hungarian Democratic Forum after its election victory obviously tends toward extreme centralization of power.[23]

Despite these worries, Antall does not have the political credentials of a Walesa or Yeltsin to establish an independent executive. Although severe economic hardship or some other major national crisis could radically alter the balance of forces between the executive and the legislative, the present tension seems healthy and inherent, not debilitating and threatening, to Hungary's democratic polity.

Hungarian Civil Society

Hungary's extended experimentation with economic reform during Communist rule allowed a degree of association outside the state not found in other Communist states. The Hungarian social contract between state and society produced an economic situation unique to Eastern Europe at the time, whereby large segments—by some estimates two-thirds—of the population dabbled to some degree in the second (i.e., capitalist) economy. Consequently, when communism collapsed in 1989, a nascent entrepreneurial class already existed.

Cleavages within society based on distinct social classes were more defined in Hungary than anywhere else in the region, giving Hungarian political parties the bases on which to build support and distinguish themselves from each other. As noted above, the Christian nationalist ideological position was quickly occupied by the Hungarian Democratic Forum, while the Alliance of Free Democrats and the smaller Federation of Young Democrats assumed the liberal side of the spectrum. The social democratic flank was represented, although initially with only limited success, by a collection of smaller parties that included the Hungarian Socialist Party (the liberal wing of the former ruling Communist Party), the Hungarian Socialist Workers' Party (a reformist Communist party), the Social Democratic Party, and the Hungarian People's Party.[24]

In sharp contrast to Russia or even Poland, where post-Communist social stratification will look very different from the classes and social groups formed under communism, Hungarian society in 1989 was already in large part reorganized according to market principles. New parties in Hungary enjoyed the luxury of identifying with social bases that would continue to exist and grow as capitalism developed. The one absent political voice may be that of workers and workers' organizations. This situation, however, is a temporary consequence of the transition from Communist rule, as the former Communists occupied and thus discredited social democratic positions during the first elections. As new social democratic parties develop untainted by Hungary's Communist past, this political position will become increasingly significant.

Moreover, because Hungary's transition was evolutionary, not revolutionary, social groups were not displaced during the transition but were given the opportunity to adjust to the new conditions of post-Communist Hungary. As Janos Kis explains,

> In Hungary, the transition was accomplished principally through negotiations; the transfer of power occurred in a mercifully quick and orderly fashion. This revolution, excluding the referendum campaign and the referendum itself, was not the product of a great popular revolt. The power of the party-state was not toppled in the streets or the work places. Mid-level officials—company, cooperative, and council leaders; judges; prosecutors; and last but not least, Communist Party functionaries—all had opportunities to reinforce their power.[25]

The nascent civil society created by Kadarization has begun to evolve to cope with the new circumstances of capitalism and democracy, but the same basic actors and social groups that formed under Kadar continue to exist today. According to one observer of democratic transitions, this continuous and spawning civil society, based not only on the old Communist order but also within an emergent capitalist system, has helped to give Hungary "the best articulated democratic political system in the post-Communist world and the most stable national government."[26]

Democratic Consolidation in Czechoslovakia

Czechoslovakia's revolutionary transition catapulted to power a new government neither known to nor elected by the majority of the republic's population. To accord his new government democratic legitimacy, Vaclav Havel called for an immediate election, in which 96 percent of the electorate voted. In the euphoria of the Velvet Revolution, Havel realized that Civic Forum and Public Against Violence were assured of electoral victory, which would then give them a popular mandate to initiate radical economic reforms. (As discussed below, the Russian democrats missed a similar opportunity to reconstitute the parliament after the August 1991 putsch.) Czechoslovakia's revolutionary transition thus mobilized voters to a much greater extent than Hungary's evolutionary transition. Havel retained his post as president while Alexander Dubcek, the leader of the 1968 Prague Spring, was elected to head the federal assembly. Civic Forum and Public Against Violence won clear majorities in their respective national councils and together won 170 out of a possible 300 seats in the federal parliament.

Because the transition in Czechoslovakia was so abrupt, parties based on different sets of social interests could not form in time for this "founding election." Instead, two new, ethnically based social movements—Civic Forum in the Czech lands and Public Against Violence in Slovakia—joined forces to wage a successful "plebiscite on communism" in this election. The antipolitics of anticommunism, however, provided for little adhesion between new Czech and Slovak political leaders. The combination of the assumption of power by these new, ethnically based movements and the almost total collapse of the Czechoslovak ancien régime propelled questions of territorial integrity to the fore in this transition.

National Unity

Unlike Poland or even Hungary, Czechoslovakia was never a nation-state but rather two nations within one state. The Czech and Slovak nations are separated geographically by identifiable borders and divided politically by separate national assemblies.[27] Their economies are also distinctive, as the Czech economy is service-oriented, industrialized, and therefore easily integrated into the international capitalist system, while Slovakia's economy is based on an unenviable combination of unproductive farms and obsolete industrial enterprises (many of them military) that were formerly closely integrated with the Soviet economy.[28] As the move to a market economy disproportionately hurt Slovakia more than the Czech Republic, economic disparities served to amplify calls for independence.[29]

Havel's strategy for dealing with separatist challenges was accommodation rather than confrontation. Symbolically, the name of the country was changed in April 1990 from the Czechoslovak Federal Republic to the Czech and Slovak Federal Republic. In December 1990, many powers previously assigned to the Federal Assembly were devolved to the Czech and Slovak national assemblies.

Slovak nationalists could not be appeased. The Slovaks initiated the process of the split, but the new Czech government quickly seized the moment to rid itself of its less developed other half. Elections in early June 1992 installed a new government in Slovakia, headed by Vladimir Meciar of the Movement for a Democratic Slovakia, that was bent on changing the constitutional arrangements of the federation. Negotiations between Meciar and Vaclav Klaus, the new prime minister of the Czech Republic, failed to preserve a federal state and instead charted a path for the peaceful separation of the Czech lands and Slovakia by 1993. On July 17, 1992, the Slovak National Assembly declared its independence. Shortly thereafter, Havel resigned as president, declaring that he would not preside over the disintegration of the Czechoslovak state. Having experienced East Central Europe's most rapid and revolutionary transition from Communist rule, Czechoslovakia has commensurately undergone the most dramatic change in state structure, culminating in the formation of two entirely new polities.

The impending split of the Czech Republic and Slovakia temporarily halted all discussion about the institutional composition of either state. Within each polity, trajectories of democratic consolidation in the context of different strategies for economic reform suggest that the Czech lands and Slovakia may develop very different kinds of democratic states, but democratic nonetheless.

The Czech Republic

Czechoslovakia's founding election was won by social movements, not political parties. Unlike movements that campaigned in elections in Poland and Russia, Civic Forum and Public Against Violence did not need to stand united in these elections because by June 1990 the Communists had already disintegrated. Rather, parties with distinct platforms and social bases had not formed in Czechoslovakia before the first elections because no period of liberalization was permitted under the former Communist regime.

As with all social movements in the region, the alliance of Civic Forum and Public Against Violence began to break apart after the collapse of the Communists. As happened in Poland, the timing and sequencing of elections in Czechoslovakia fostered an unstable, disintegrative process. Because the first elections in the

Republic were contests between the old Communists and the *fronts*, the second round of elections—after two years of economic hardship—gave birth to several dozen new parties. For the June 1992 elections, there were more than 80 parties vying for a position on the ballot.[30]

Within Civic Forum, the main split erupted along ideological lines regarding economic reform and anti-Communist nationalism.[31] Vaclav Klaus, then the first Czechoslovak finance minister, spearheaded the formation of the Interparliamentary Group of the Democratic Right, a group that attracted 57 Civic Forum deputies at its formation on October 10, 1990, and later constituted the basis of the right-of-center political grouping called the Civic Democratic Party. Before the June 1992 elections, the Civic Democratic Party signed a coalition agreement with the Christian Democratic Union—People's Party to consolidate the right side of the Czech Republic's political spectrum. As Klaus declared, this new alliance has a common enemy, "which is to the left of us . . . and not only the Communist Party, but also social democracy, the Liberal Social Party, and the nationalist Moravian parties."[32] This coalition of right-wing parties closely reflects traditional right-of-center parties in the West in that it combines laissez-faire economic advocacy with strong state nationalism. As finance minister, Klaus organized the most comprehensive privatization packages in the region, explaining that "the early, rapid transformation of property rights is absolutely crucial for the reform to succeed."[33] Klaus, his Civic Democratic Party, and his coalition of right-of-center parties were the clear winners in the June 1992 elections, making Klaus the new prime minister.[34]

To the left of Klaus's coalition, Jiri Dienstbier, a leading Civic Forum activist and the first post-Communist foreign minister of Czechoslovakia, founded first the Liberal Club and finally the Civic Movement Party. Civic Movement has tried to define itself as a centrist party with liberal democratic views. Groups such as Obroda, the Left Alternative, and the Club of Social Democrats have espoused more traditional social democratic causes.

The left flank of the Czech political spectrum, excluding the former Communist Party and its manifestations, is occupied by the Czechoslovak Social Democracy, the Liberal Social Union (which includes the Agrarian Party, the Socialist Party, and the

Green Party), and the Communist Party of Bohemia and Moravia. All these parties have spoken out against privatization and warned against German colonization.

Although fragile, the coalition government represents a unified set of parties and interests. Political parties in the Czech Republic, in fact, have consolidated around three major coalitions all apparently committed to the parliamentary process. Carefully crafted election laws have helped the Czech Republic avoid the level of parliamentary division experienced in post-Solidarity Poland.[35] Finally, rapid economic growth and a successful transition to a market economy have stimulated the formation of a new and vibrant independent civil society in the Czech Republic. The deleterious consequences of rapid revolutionary change have been offset by a relatively easy transition to the market and shrewd political decisions about the timing and sequencing of elections.

Slovakia

In Slovakia, differences between political parties emerging after the collapse of Public Against Violence have been defined by the degree of support for Slovakian independence and commensurate intolerance for minorities living in Slovakia. The most nationalist political group, the Slovak National Party, has advocated immediate Slovak independence and campaigned for Slovak to be the official language of Slovakia. Although capturing only 15 seats in the June 1992 elections, this party has succeeded in pushing the terms of the debate about independence increasingly to the right.

The more nationalist wing of Public Against Violence has coalesced around the leadership of Vladimir Meciar and the new Movement for a Democratic Slovakia. Commenting on calls from the Slovak National Party for complete independence before the June elections, Meciar remarked, "The sovereignty of numerous countries is being recognized in Europe at the moment. I see no reason why this should not be possible in our case as well."[36] Like many parties in other East European countries (and unlike traditional West European parties), the Movement for a Democratic Slovakia combines Christian nationalism (separatism) with a cautious approach to economic reform. This approach distinguishes Slovak conservatism from right-wing parties in the Czech

Republic, which have coupled nationalism (federalism) with support for rapid privatization and market creation. As Meciar
explained, "We advocate a market economy and pluralism of the
forms of ownership. However, the limits of what our people can
endure have been reached."[37] This is a particularly potent combination in Slovakia, as the swift shift to capitalism has had more
adverse effects there than in the Czech Republic. Jiri Musil has
gone one step further to argue that Slovaks are culturally less suit-
ed for capitalism than the Czechs: "Most differences . . . are caused
by the fact that in the building of the new state, Czech society in
its majority prefers civic and individualistic principles; the
Slovaks favor national and solidaristic ones."[38]

   Closer to the middle of the Slovak political spectrum, Jan
Carnogursky founded the more moderate yet still nationalistic
Christian Democratic Movement (CDM), which was never a member of Public Against Violence. The CDM joined Public Against
Violence to form Slovakia's first government after the June 1990
elections; Meciar, for Public Against Violence, became prime minister while Carnogursky became first Slovak deputy prime minister. Initially the CDM supported a federal treaty, but the increasing
popularity of calls for Slovakian independence has shifted the
entire party to the right. Although careful to warn against the damaging consequences of "sudden independence," as early as 1990,
Carnogursky supported a new Slovak constitution that would
allow Slovakia to "leave the federation if [the Slovaks'] ideas and
requirements are not fulfilled."[39]

   Firmly situated to the left of center is the new Social
Democratic Party, which was headed by Alexander Dubcek until
his death. Although sharing Meciar's concern about the adverse
effects of a rapid transition to a market economy, the social
democrats have advocated the preservation of the federation.
They are joined in issues of both the state and the economy by the
remnants of the old Communist Party, now called the Party of the
Democratic Left.

   The June 1992 elections established a clear mandate for
Meciar and his Movement for a Democratic Slovakia. His movement captured 74 out of 150 seats in the parliament, followed by
the Party of the Democratic Left (29 seats), the Christian
Democratic Movement (18 seats), the Slovak National Party (15

seats), and the ethnically based Coexistence/Hungarian Christian Democratic Movement (14 seats).[40] With only five parties represented in parliament, one of them with a significant plurality, Slovakia's newly elected government may be more secure than any other in the region. Moreover, a basic level of consensus about economic policy among Slovakia's major parties will contribute to a stable and effective government. The pace of reform unquestionably will slow, the role of the state will be significant, and the consequent emerging civil society will be shaped more in accord with past Communist social stratifications. In other words, the old Communist *nomenklatura* will play a much greater role in determining government policy and acquiring new private properties. The vast majority of Slovakia's political parties, however, supported by a recent popular election, seem to want this kind of polity. Although different from the Czech Republic, Slovakia's polity appears, thus far, to be no less democratic.

3
Russia's Transition from Communism

Compared with Poland, Czechoslovakia, or Hungary, Russia began the process of liberalization under Gorbachev with the least developed civil society, the most far-reaching state-party apparat, and the least inspiring history on which to ground, model, or legitimate new democratic organizations and institutions. Beginning with the Communist Party and ending with stamp collecting clubs, the Soviet regime penetrated and controlled virtually all associational activity beyond the family. Josef Stalin tried to destroy the family unit as well, but this ultimate manifestation of the totalitarian state was abandoned under Nikita Khrushchev.

In this atmosphere of extreme state mobilization and manipulation of social life, even seemingly innocuous social formations such as football fan clubs or Russian cultural groups were considered threats to the state. Although dissidents did organize and occasionally act, these isolated events never triggered a massive political uprising such as occurred in Hungary in 1956, Czechoslovakia in 1968, or Poland in 1980–1981. In contrast to its East European colonies, the Soviet totalitarian state was relatively successful. Whether one considers the Soviet system totalitarian, authoritarian, or post-totalitarian, it does appear that the *intentions* of the Soviet state were to have total control of all political, economic, and, to a lesser degree, social activity.[1]

The lack of a civil society, and the absence of even an influential group within society advocating the formation of a "second society," accorded Russia a special starting point in moving away from authoritarian rule. Most obviously, the initial push for change came from above, not below. Describing such regimes as "liberalized authoritarianism," Guillermo O'Donnell and Philippe Schmitter have noted in other transitions that

authoritarian rulers may tolerate or even promote liberalization in the belief that by opening up certain spaces for
individual and group action, they can relieve various pressures and obtain needed information and support *without*
altering the structure of authority, that is, without becom-
ing accountable to the citizenry for their actions or sub-
jecting their claim to rule to fair and competitive elections.[2]

Although he later would try to shut the lid on the very social
forces he has unleashed, Gorbachev nonetheless almost single-
handedly launched political liberalization in the Soviet Union.

Once *glasnost* (openness) and *demokratizatsia* (democratization) allowed for social and political activity outside of the state,
the kind of actors emanating from Russia's nascent civil society
reflected the peculiar Soviet legacy. Whereas the leadership of
East Central Europe's new political movements all had established reputations as dissidents outside of state-party structures,
the vast majority of Russia's "democratic" leaders were
Communist Party members with distinctly nondissident back-
grounds.[3] While Czechoslovakia's opposition hero, Vaclav Havel,
was a playwright and Poland's leading figure, Lech Walesa, was an
electrician, Boris Yeltsin, the leader of Russia's democratic movement, was a former first secretary and a candidate Politburo member in the CPSU. Because the Soviet Communist Party and state
had so permeated Russian society while violently repressing all
those who tried to resist, almost all future democratic leaders had
to be drawn from CPSU ranks.[4]

The Soviet state's relative success at capturing and controlling
all economic, political, and social activity meant that the eventual
articulation of anti-Soviet sentiment would be initially collectivist
and amorphous rather than particularist or defined.[5] The state
acted to eliminate classes and social groups, relegating everyone
to two basic categories—"them" (the Communist Party *nomenklatura*) and "us" (everyone else). Although this kind of social
structure emerged in other Communist regimes in Eastern
Europe, the lack of class and group cleavages within Soviet society
was particularly acute.

Moreover, because Russia's experience with civil society was
short-lived and long ago and the intellectual or dissident commit-

ment to the idea of the separation of state and society was either weak or poorly understood, initial independent political associations tended to be very state-centric. Rather than seeking to carve out alternative and separate spaces from the state, Russia's successful social movements focused their energies on influencing and later capturing the state. (Contrast this strategy with Solidarity's tactic of creating a civil society independent of the state.) Perhaps as a legacy of 70 years of reading and reciting Leninist scriptures, even the most radical anti-Communists still believed that revolutionary change could only be undertaken by using the state (and not, for instance, social groups or economic activity outside of the state's purview) to bulldoze into place a new social order.

These particular legacies of Soviet history influenced both the mode of Russia's revolutionary transition and the form of post-Communist consolidation of Russia's new, and still forming, polity.

The Period of Informals

As noted, the Communist Party of the Soviet Union, in its constitutional capacity as the "leading and guiding force" in Soviet society (Article Six of the USSR Constitution), squashed all elements of independent political activity for much of its 70-year tenure in power. Gorbachev's regime allowed for the first sprouts of organized, politicized civil society, which later erupted into movements, parties, and fronts bent on destroying the old order. Initially, these groups organized around specific and relatively nonpolitical issues, such as the environment, Russian cultural renewal, or rock music. Very quickly, however, several organizations and factions within apolitical groups began to assume increasingly overt political profiles. The evolution of *Club Lingua* and *Nash Arbat* are two examples. By 1988, a political spectrum was already discernible.

The most overtly political product of Gorbachev's liberalization and *glasnost* was the Democratic Union, a coalition of several different ideological tendencies ranging from neo-Thatcherism to Eurocommunism but all dedicated to the destruction of Soviet communism. An outgrowth of the "Democracy and Humanism" seminar of former dissidents and new, young activists, the Democratic Union became a political party in May 1988, the first of a new generation of Russian political parties in almost 70 years.[6] Although ideologically heterogenous about the future, Democratic Union activists became famous for their militant and united appeal for democracy and, commensurately, the destruction of the CPSU. To achieve these ends, the Democratic Union unabashedly employed confrontational tactics, including marches on KGB (State Security Committee) headquarters and anti-Gorbachev and anti-*perestroika* (restructuring) rallies in Pushkin Square.[7] After the invasion of Lithuania and Latvia in January 1991, a faction within the Democratic Union led by Valeriia Novodvorskaia even advocated the use of violence in self-defense against the Soviet totalitarian regime.[8]

Taking their cue from Gorbachev's call for a more open political dialogue, first publicists and later young academicians, *raikom* (district committee) party bosses, and instructors of scientific socialism organized political clubs to discuss the Soviet reform process. Although dozens formed and dissolved, some of the most famous *neformaly* (informal) organizations of this era included the Club of Socialist Initiative (KSI), *Klub Perestroika* (in Moscow and Leningrad), Democratic *Perestroika*, *Perestroika* 88, *Obshchina* (Commune), *Grazhdanskoe Dostoinstvo* (Civic Dignity), the All-Union Socio-Political Club (VSPK), and the Federation of Socialist Social Clubs (FSOK).[9] The nuclei of several future parties, as well as many of the future leaders of Russia's parliament and government, participated in these discussion forums. Unlike the Democratic Union, these groups avoided direct confrontation with the Soviet regime. Many of their discussion groups were housed in Communist Party buildings. Similarly, many participants were CPSU members. Although increasingly disillusioned with the objectives of *perestroika*, these clubs and associations nonetheless advocated tactics of compromise and policies of incremental change. Revolution was not an agenda item.

Reactionary nationalist organizations, including most notably the dozen *Pamyat'* (Memory) groups, constituted a third political current to emerge in these early years of *glasnost*. In sharp contrast to either the Democratic Union or the pro-*perestroika* groups, these groups opposed both communism and democracy. Both ideologies, they asserted, were Jewish, Western, and Zionist, alien to the true spirit of Russia.[10] Salvation, they claimed, could

only be attained by returning to the Russian lifestyle of the nineteenth century. These reactionary organizations never crystallized
into a unified, all-federation movement, but every region and city
had its own local nationalist group by the end of the decade.

Communism as a mobilizing ideology also appeared somewhat
later than these other trends within Soviet civil society. Allegedly,
this political force also emerged from below, beginning with Nina
Andreeva's letter called "I Cannot Give up My Principles," which
was published in March 1988 in *Sovetskaya Rossiya*.[11] The letter
constituted an ideological treatise for conservative Communists
who were upset with the direction of Gorbachev's reforms and led
to the creation of the neo-Stalinist group *Edinstvo* (Unity).[12] The
following year, the conservative Communist organization the
United Workers' Front held its founding congress in Leningrad,
thereby establishing, at least theoretically, a Communist social
movement not controlled by the state or party.[13] The core founders
of the United Workers' Front were all members of the CPSU, but
the top leadership of the Communist Party did not condone the
formation of this neo-Communist organization.

Elections, Polarization, Revolution

The Nineteenth Party Conference in 1988, elections for the
Congress of People's Deputies of the USSR in 1989, and especially
the election process for deputies to the Russian Congress of
People's Deputies, coupled with elections for local and district
councils, provided major catalysts for mobilization of Russia's
emerging democratic forces. The wider the franchise for these
elections, the more mobilized Russian society became. During the
Nineteenth Party Conference, the pro-*perestroika* clubs and civic
groups organized the first sanctioned series of public demonstrations not orchestrated by the Communist Party.[14] Although the
party conference was a strictly Communist affair, independent
civic groups such as *Obshchina* and *Grazhdanskoe Dostoinstvo*
conducted weekly meetings in Pushkin Square during May and
June 1988 as a means of influencing the conference's agenda.
Because the Communist Party was still synonymous with the
Soviet state at this stage, lobbying the party conference represented a major moment in opening a space between the Soviet state
and Russian society.

An important, unintended consequence of the political activity surrounding the Nineteenth Party Conference was the formation of popular fronts in major cities throughout Russia. Modeled after the Estonian Popular Front, these fronts represented a major step toward consolidation of new political forces outside the state and party. In Moscow, the idea of creating a Moscow Popular Front first arose in June 1988 and was formalized at a conference of informal groups and associations organized by the Federation of Socialist Social Clubs and the All-Union Socio-Political Club on August 21, 1988. In the fall, the Moscow Popular Front elected a coordinating committee, which then organized a founding congress on March 2, 1989.[15] Powerful fronts had also been organized in Leningrad, Yaroslavl', Stavropol, and Khabarovsk. Inspired by grass-roots activity in other cities, which at this stage often exceeded the work of informals in the capital, front organizers in Moscow and Leningrad even began to plan and organize an All-Russian Popular Front.[16]

Popular fronts in Moscow and elsewhere still lacked an ideology in opposition to the basic principles of Gorbachev's *perestroika*. The Moscow Popular Front passed a hotly contested resolution at its first organizational meeting espousing democratic socialism.[17] Although old revolutionary slogans such as "All Power to the Soviets" and "Land for the Peasants" were resurrected as an obvious affront to the CPSU-state bureaucracy, the 1989 Moscow Popular Front Charter still listed "respect for ideals, peace, free democracy, and socialism" as its principal concerns.[18] At this juncture, debating the merits of socialism was still not central to the agenda for these popular fronts. The Moscow Popular Front did take some positions regarding specific policies, such as support for the development of cooperatives and "democratization of the state and social life."[19] It never challenged the course of *perestroika* directly, however. Rather, the focus of activity was still support for reform, however vaguely defined, as carried out by the system in place.

Frustrated by his inability to mobilize his Communist Party into a vanguard for radical economic reform, Gorbachev tried to extract the state from the party by creating the Congress of People's Deputies. Although the Communist Party, the *Komsomol*, the official trade unions, and several other social organizations dominated by the CPSU were allotted seats, many of the local CPSU functionaries had to face elections to become deputies in the Congress.

Election procedures still blocked the nomination of most "radical democrats," the term then used to describe those political figures pressing for rapid political reform. Nonetheless, the process itself mobilized mass popular participation into voters' associations, campaign organizations, and support groups for individual candidates. Although only one candidate produced from the "informals," Sergei Stankevich, won election to the Congress, independent voters' associations did help elect several progressive candidates (both in popular elections and in elections held within public organizations), including Yurii Afanasiev, Telman Gdlyan, Arkadii Murashev, Andrei Sakharov, and Ilya Zaslavskii. Perhaps even more important, voters' associations and popular fronts succeeded in conducting negative campaigns against senior figures from the CPSU hierarchy.[20]

Independent political mobilization grew throughout 1989 as live television coverage of the Congress of People's Deputies continually injected new issues for discussion and protest. The objective of political activity at this stage still remained confined to prodding reform within the system. Within the Congress hall, advocates of radical reform organized the Interregional Deputies' Group to spur reform from within. Outside of the Congress, the Moscow Popular Front and *Memorial*, a social group dedicated to commemorating the victims of Stalinism, hosted almost daily mass meetings near Luzhniki stadium to influence the course of reform *within* the parliament and the party-state administrative apparatus as a whole. Attacks on the Communist command system became increasingly virulent, but the vast majority of new political actions both within and outside of the party-state focused on criticizing and reforming the old rather than creating something new.

Antipolitics reached its zenith during the elections in March 1990 for the Russian Congress of People's Deputies as well as local and district councils. By this time, democrats no longer believed that the ancien régime could be reformed. At the same time, they realized that their independent political formations were not capable of dismantling the entrenched party-state system at the

Union level. As a strategy for dealing with this balance of forces, advocates of radical reform sought to seize control of state institutions through the electoral process. These reinvigorated structures of the state then would implement radical reform at the lowest levels of government. The old order at the top simply would be ignored.

Anticommunism, anti-status quo, and even anti-Gorbachev were the themes propagated to gain control of the state organs during the 1990 elections. This common "ideology of opposition" helped to create the Democratic Russia bloc, a coalition of candidates running against the old order.[21] This organization stretched across the entire Russian Republic, uniting almost all non-Communist and nonfascist political clubs, groups, and associations. Although elections in the provinces yielded councils still dominated by Communist Party apparatchiks, Democratic Russia did win clear majorities in the Moscow and Leningrad city councils, as well as a near majority in the Russian Congress of People's Deputies.

Elections in 1989 and especially in 1990 catalyzed only anti-Communist, democratically oriented political organizations and especially the Democratic Russia bloc. These stimulants for democratically oriented organizations did not activate a commensurate growth for either nationalists or neo-Communists. For activists and, eventually, voters seeking to totally reject the old order, democracy and the market served as the most effective ideologies of opposition when juxtaposed to the Communist system. Both of these ideas were polar opposites of the Soviet command system and therefore offered a clearly defined alternative to the status quo. These ideas also were associated with the successful models of capitalist democracy in Western Europe and the United States. To be democratic was to be Western, was to be American, was to be wealthy.

At this point, other ideologies could not compete. Neo-Communist groups were identified too much with the past, while even pro-*perestroika* socialist and social democratic organizations eventually had to abandon (at least temporarily) all discourse vaguely associated with the ancien régime. The platform of the Social Democratic Party of Russia (SPDR), for instance, was far more "right-wing" than its Western social democratic counterparts.[22]   In espousing a strong, imperial state, nationalist and patriotic organizations also alienated a society exhausted from 70 years of "superpowerness." Moreover, neither neocommunism nor neonationalism (nor just plain nationalism) could point to successful examples of their models. Even if they could, none had access to mass media to let others know about it. At this stage, the battle lines were drawn between the "democrats" created by popular support within society and the "Communists" entrenched in the state.

Democrats "Seize the State"

The democrats' strategy of translating anti-Communist societal support into state power did not work. Even in those city councils where democrats held a majority, they rarely organized to pass significant legislation. Although most of the new people's deputies from the democratic camp were loosely affiliated with the Democratic Russia bloc, this coalition lacked discipline, cohesion, and a single political platform. New political parties, which formed as a result of the repeal of Article Six of the Soviet Constitution in February 1990, had organized too late to participate in the March 1990 elections. Consequently, few people's deputies had party affiliations (other than the Communist Party), and those who did join parties did not feel obligated to vote along party lines. When candidates run in elections on party platforms, they owe some allegiance to that platform and the party for winning their seat. When, as in the Russian case, a parliamentarian joins a (weak) party after being elected independently, that party has few carrots or sticks to induce party discipline. The result was intense debate—a healthy sign of a democratic process—but few concrete actions.

Yet, even if the democrats had been better organized, they had inherited a set of government institutions that were never designed to govern. For most of the USSR's existence, real creation and execution of policy were handled by the Communist Party. The Politburo, not the USSR Supreme Soviet, defined policy, while the district (*raikom*) Communist Party branch, not the local city council, ensured that Politburo decisions were executed. The executive committees (*ispolkomy*) of the councils did implement decisions of the Communist Party (rubber-stamped by the council). These committees were composed almost entirely of people from the local Communist Party committee, however, and of course were neither elected by the people nor appointed by the council.

Elections in 1990 for councils at all levels gave these state institutions new legitimacy to govern but little real power to govern effectively. The sheer number of deputies in each council (500 people's deputies in the Moscow City Council, 200 in the average city borough or *raikom*), the lack of clear division between executive and legislative power, and the absence of jurisdictional demarcations between district, city, oblast, republic, and Union, all combined to paralyze effective government at all levels.[23] As Moscow mayor Gavriil Popov concluded, "It would be an utter delusion to think that a complete rebuilding of the USSR can be done without changing today's Soviet system whose basic features were formed in 1917. Our political system is as outdated as our command economy."[24]

Even if the Soviet system had been reorganized, this set of government bodies still coexisted within the USSR command economy controlled by the Communist Party. This system was collapsing, but it had not withered entirely. Although the ancien régime may have been too weak at this stage to *initiate* change itself, it still had the capacity to *block* reform initiated elsewhere. At the local level, conflicts between the Moscow City Council and the Union-level, party-state apparatus resulted in food blockades of the capital as well as an irreconcilable dispute over the appointment of the city's police chief.[25]   At the federal level, the attempt at cohabitation between Yeltsin's Russia and Gorbachev's Soviet Union fueled the "war of laws" during the fall of 1990. Democrats had "seized the state," but only in a handful of places and only that part of the state that wielded little to no power.

The Birth of Political Parties and the New, Improved Democratic Russia

Paralysis of power in the councils, coupled with an increasingly conservative government surrounding Gorbachev at the Union level, propelled the Russian "transition" into an extremely polarized situation. Unlike nonrevolutionary transitions, in which the terms of the transition are either dictated by authoritarian rulers or negotiated between the authoritarian regime (and usually with the "soft-liners" within that regime) and proponents of democratic rule, the Russian transition had reached a stalemate by 1991. Democratic challengers and the Soviet Union's old guard held antithetical conceptions of the state and economy. This predicament mobilized Russia's political forces into two clearly defined camps, leaving little room for third parties or compromise agendas.

In this situation, institutions and organizations commonly associated with functioning democracies, like political parties, civic groups, or other intermediaries between the state and society, played only a marginal role. The Democratic Party of Russia, the Social Democratic Party of Russia, the Republican Party of Russia, and a handful of other Christian democratic and constitutional democratic parties were all founded during 1990, but none grew to play a significant role in Russia's revolutionary transition. During revolutionary situations in which conflicts become polarized between forces that are competing for ultimate sovereignty and thus do not agree on the basic rules of political competition, both sides have an interest in maintaining political unity and ideological unanimity. Pluralism serves neither side. Moreover, given Russia's amorphous socioeconomic structure in limbo between a command system and a market economy, none of these new political parties had solid social bases of support.[26] Finally, Russia's exhaustion with the very word *party* after 70 years of Party rule further hindered party development.

Those political parties that did form during this period were compelled to unite under the banner of the revived "Democratic Russia" Movement, which held its founding congress as a movement (rather than as an election bloc) in October 1990. Although parties originally may have considered Democratic Russia to be a coalition of parties and other political associations, the movement as a whole soon assumed the role of the leading opposition group, diluting the voice of individual parties' interests in the greater task of defeating communism.[27] Beginning in January 1991 with a protest over the invasions of Lithuania and Latvia, the Democratic Russia Movement organized a series of mass actions in response to Gorbachev's increasingly conservative actions. This period of street mobilization culminated on March 28, 1991, when hundreds of thousands of Democratic Russia activists throughout

Russia defied Gorbachev's ban on demonstrations to show their support for Yeltsin. At the time, conservative forces within the Russian Congress of People's Deputies had launched a campaign to relieve Yeltsin of his duties as chairman of the Russian parliament.

The crescendo of popular anti-Soviet sentiment throughout the spring and summer of 1991 culminated in the landslide election of Yeltsin as Russia's first president on June 12 and dramatically shifted the balance of forces between the old and new. Sensing this shift, even Gorbachev agreed to deal with Yeltsin and the "radical democrats" by signing the "9 + 1 Accord," the penultimate step toward a new Union treaty. At this stage, it appeared that Russia's transition might be negotiated and peaceful.

Gorbachev may have resigned himself to dealing with Yeltsin, a new Russian government, and a new relationship between the "center" and the "republics," but his conservative government did not.[28] On August 19, 1991, the latter made a desperate and pathetic attempt to restore the Soviet ancien régime. The effort failed miserably. Paradoxically, in attempting to restore the status quo, the August coup radically transformed the pace and process of Russia's revolutionary transition. Yeltsin's new government did not have to face negotiating, compromising, and coexisting with opponents from the old system. Instead, the collapse of the Soviet Union and the retreat of the conservative Communist guard bestowed Yeltsin and his government with a *temporary* tabula rasa for creating a new Russian polity.

4
State Building in Post-Communist Russia

The first stage of Russia's transition from Communist, authoritarian rule was revolutionary and dramatic, culminating in the emotional climax of the failed August 1991 coup. Although the sudden, accelerated rejection of communism might seem conducive to radical and rapid democratic reform, the essential next step, the consolidation of democracy, is proving extremely difficult. Russia lags behind East Central Europe in overcoming three critical issues in the transition from authoritarian rule to the consolidation of a democratic state. First, the territorial integrity of the Russian state has yet to be decided. Unlike Poland or Hungary, the Russian nation and the Russian state are not synonymous. The collapse of the Soviet imperial state has left Russian expatriates in former colonies. Even the territoriality of the multiethnic Russian Federation is in doubt. Unlike Czechoslovakia's leaders, Russian politicians have not even articulated options for resolving these border conflicts, much less chosen among them.[1]

Second, the structure of government is still very elastic. The banning of the Communist Party in August 1991 and the dissolution of the Soviet Union in December of that year demolished the two main administrative organs of the old Soviet order. In the new Russian state, neither the division of power among the legislative, executive, and judiciary branches nor the demarcation of authority between different levels of government has been established. Consequently, regular procedures have not been institutionalized regarding any aspect of governance. Lawmaking itself occurs ad hoc, and its results are often eclipsed by presidential decrees or undermined by individual actions.

Third, the definition of the borders, structures, and processes of the Russian state is taking place in the context of a society and economy in total flux. The concurrent transformation of both the Russian polity and the socioeconomic system has challenged tra-

ditional articulations of class and social group interests, undermined former societal stratifications, and even destroyed the
bases of newly formed "democratic" alliances and organizations.
With the simplistic dichotomy of "democrat" versus "Communist"
now removed, Russia's emerging civic groups have begun to reor-
ganize and disorganize according to new conditions of post-
Communist Russian society. The kinds of civic organizations that
formed during the polarized period of opposition politics may no
longer be effective in articulating, representing, or aggregating
public interests in the new Russia. Political parties, one of the
most important intermediaries between state and society in stable
democracies, are still weak and ineffectual, impeded in their
development by Russia's fluid political and economic situation as
well as by the lack of opportunities—first and foremost elections—
to extend their political importance. Other types of socioeconomic organizations such as lobbies, trade unions, or interest groups
are only beginning to mature. Few of these social units have a
rational self-interest in promoting market reforms and therefore
may use democratic processes to abort government plans for creating a capitalist system. Although other East European countries
face similar dilemmas, the scale in Russia dwarfs all others.

Where Is Russia?

In mapping a path from the end of the transition from totalitarian
rule to the beginning of democratic consolidation, Russia's new
leaders first must define the state within which social forces
(movements, parties, or individuals) can compete democratically
to gain power and influence outcomes. At the most basic level, the
first set of questions that must be resolved about a state concerns
the demarcation of borders, boundaries, and sovereignty.

As early as the summer of 1990, Russia declared its independence as a sovereign state. Real definition of the territorial integrity of this sovereign state really began, however, after the collapse
of the Soviet Union. The process has proved difficult and dangerous. The Russian nation is not located neatly within the borders of
the Russian state. Moreover, hundreds of non-Russian peoples are
contained within the Russian state, while still others are located
on both sides of Russia's borders. To create a new Russian state,
Russia's new leaders must first demarcate where Russia ends and
where *blizhnii zarubezh* (near abroad) begins.

Russia's boundaries are most poorly defined in the Crimea, Moldova, and the Caucasus. Vice President Aleksandr Rutskoi and others have argued that Ukraine must return the Crimea to Russia. Stimulated by this debate, the Crimean Supreme Soviet created the independent Republic of Crimea in May 1992. The following month, the Republican Movement of the Crimea vowed to fight for independence even if Ukraine constructed a total blockade.[2]

At the same time, ethnic Russians in the Transdniestr Republic of Moldova have called for independence from Moldova and are supported by several prominent Russian political leaders and institutions (Rutskoi, Stankevich, and even the Moscow City Council), especially after the Moldovan bombing of Bendery during the summer of 1992, in which several hundred Russians were killed. After the bombings, the chairman of the Transdniestr parliament, Grigorii Marakutsa declared, "After the savage operation in Bendery we shall not maintain our relations with Moldova on a federation basis. Transdniestr will fight for complete independence."[3] Subsequently, Dniestr Republic President Igor Smirnov announced plans for the creation of a Dniestr army, while the resident commander of Russia's 14th Army, General Aleksandr Lebed, has vowed to defend at whatever cost Russians living in the region. Even Ukrainian President Leonid Kravchuk said that Transdniestr should be granted autonomous status within Moldova and full independence if Moldova and Romania merge

In the Caucasus, Southern Ossetians have petitioned to join the Russian Federation to unite their people and to escape Georgia.[4] In October 1992, Yeltsin declared a state of emergency in this area and appointed his deputy prime minister, Sergei Shakhrai, as the local head of government. None of these border disputes has been resolved.

Meanwhile, within Russia's borders, self-determination, one of the very issues that mobilized Russia's anti-Communist movement in 1990–1991 and spawned the new Russian state, now threatens to partition Russia itself. The devolution of power that eventually destroyed the Soviet Union has continued, unabated, to stimulate independence movements in several non-Russian "autonomous regions" as well as a handful of ethnically Russian oblasts tired of Moscow's domination.

The growing significance of these independence movements—particularly in Tatarstan and Chechen-Ingushetiya—often
stems as much from Moscow's vastly weakened central authority
as it does from the actual appeal of independence in these
regions. The governmental structure of the Russian Federation
was never designed to govern. Crafted under Stalin, the concentric
circles of different ethnically based territories within the federation and the Soviet Union as a whole established a rationale for
Communist subjugation of other states. Under Moscow's strong
central authority during the Communist era, even grumblings of
pro-independence sentiment were quickly squashed. The super-
imposition of the Communist Party organization over this complex federative administration established the real channels of
power, even if they often paralleled the ostensible governmental
structure.

When the Soviet state and Communist Party disintegrated,
local authorities seized the moment to assert control.[5]   In many
regions, these struggles between center and periphery are exacerbated by the imbalanced Communist quotient between the war-
ring camps. In the autonomous regions, most of the independence
leaders are local Communist warlords, who had supported the
Union as a buffer against Russian imperialism and who now resist
radical economic reform as a threat to their fiefdoms.

Chechen-Ingushetiya has led the rush to claim independence
and sovereignty, prompting Yeltsin to issue a state of emergency in
the region that included military occupation. On March 12, 1992,
the Chechen parliament decreed that the Chechen Republic was
an independent secular state. The legislative body has taken initial
steps toward defining Chechen citizenship and approved prepara-
tions for a local currency. Anticipating Russia's reaction to these
measures, Chechen President Dzhakhar Dudayev warned that
"there will be war and it will not be limited to our republic. We
have good contacts and agreements with other republics in the
Caucasus. The recent events have shown us that tens of thousands
of soldiers from all over the Caucasus are ready to fight against
Russia."[6] Increased fighting in August and September in this
region prompted Yeltsin to declare another state of emergency in
the Ingush Republic and the North Ossetian Republic, an act that
transferred all administrative authority to a Russian government

official. Initially, Deputy Prime Minister Georgii Khizha was named the local head of administration in this disputed region. (Sergei Shakhrai replaced him in November.) In response, Dudayev asserted that the decision "proves the falsity of the policy of the Russian leadership and the colonial nature of the federative treaty."[7]

Tatarstan also has threatened to secede. Although still lacking the intensity of the Chechen-Ingushetiya campaign, the independence movement in Tatarstan climaxed in March 1992, when a referendum declaring the republic's independence was supported by more than 60 percent of the population.[8] After the elections, Tatarstan President Mintimer Shaimiev did proclaim his willingness to negotiate with Russia about Tatarstan's status, but he also asserted that the referendum was a higher authority than the Constitutional Court, that Tatarstan would not sign Yeltsin's new federal treaty, and that his government would pay federal taxes only for services rendered directly to his republic. Most recently, the Tatarstan government has claimed ownership of all state property in the republic and has issued its own vouchers to privatize these properties. Shaimiev and other Tatar leaders want to reach a special settlement with Russia for Tatarstan to remain outside of the framework of the federation treaty yet within the bounds of the Russian state. Nonetheless, initial steps toward full independence, coupled with Moscow's inability to focus on the Tatarstan problem, create inauspicious conditions for a solution in the near term. Tatarstan may end up being to Russia what Lithuania was to the Soviet Union. Tatarstan's strategic location and valuable natural resources make the consequences of its secession much more serious for Russia than a Chechen-Ingushetiya departure.

In lieu of a new constitution, Yeltsin drafted and negotiated a "Treaty on Demarcating Spheres of Jurisdiction and Powers Between the Russian Federation's Federal Organs of State Power and the Organs of Power of the Russian Federation's Constituent Republics," which 18 of the 20 republics signed. The content of the treaty will become part of the constitution when it is adopted. The signing of this treaty, coupled with Yeltsin's new strategy of conscious and quiet neglect of independence declarations, arrested temporarily the degeneration of the Russian Republic.[9] In the spring of 1993, however, leaders from the autonomous regions launched a new campaign for greater autonomy from Moscow, claiming that the Russian federal government had failed to deliver on responsibilities and commitments outlined in the federal treaty. Disputes over the demarcation of federal and republic powers will continue to threaten the consolidation of Russia's democracy until all parties have vested interests in a new federal system.

Defining the Government: The Division of Horizontal Power

Yeltsin and the Executive Branch

After several months of indecision immediately following the coup, Russian president Boris Yeltsin moved to fill the political vacuum created by the collapse of the Communist Party, and later the Soviet Union itself, with a newly constructed executive structure. Before the coup, Yeltsin and his associates already had begun to strengthen executive power through the creation of a Russian presidency and mayoral offices in Moscow and Leningrad (later renamed St. Petersburg). The offices of the Russian presidency and the Moscow mayor were created by referenda held on March 17, 1991, the same day Soviet citizens voted on whether to preserve the Soviet Union. After the coup, as explained in detail below, Yeltsin created by decree new executive offices— *glavy administratsii* (heads of administration)—at every level of government.

During the fall of 1991, Yeltsin also secured from the parliament the power to issue executive decrees. The presidential orders were to be the legal equivalent of laws passed by the parliament. Yeltsin regarded executive power, not parliament or social movements, as the engine of economic and political transformation. For this reason, he neglected to form or revamp other political institutions. Most significantly, he did not seek to create a political party in support of his revolutionary agenda, and he did not call for new elections for legislative organs at a time when his supporters surely would have won majorities. Retrospectively, this may have been his greatest mistake.

To strengthen executive power at the highest levels of government, Yeltsin created a dual system of executive power, one formal and one informal. The formal structure, the government (*pravitel'stvo*), resembled many other European governments, complete with a prime minister, deputy prime ministers, and ministers.[10] In Russia's first post-Communist government, Yeltsin appointed himself prime minister and named three deputy prime ministers—Yegor Gaidar, Gennadii Burbulis, and Aleksandr Shokhin. According to the amended Soviet constitution still in effect, this government was to be appointed by the president but approved by the parliament, the Congress of People's Deputies.

Within the executive branch of government, however, Yeltsin established a series of offices and institutions not accountable to the parliament. Yeltsin picked a handful of advisers, later named state councillors, who reported directly to the president. Being outside of the *pravitel'stvo*, these "advisers" could not be removed by the legislative branch of government, the Congress of People's Deputies. For instance, Yeltsin appointed Yegor Gaidar as his personal economic adviser after Gaidar failed to gain parliamentary approval as prime minister.

Even more informally, Yeltsin surrounded himself with a handful of long-time personal aides commonly referred to as the "Sverdlovsk mafia." Yurii Petrov, Yeltsin's chief of staff, had served as second first secretary of the Sverdlovsk Communist Party when Yeltsin was first secretary. Viktor Iliushin, chief of secretariat, was first secretary of the Sverdlovsk oblast *Komsomol*. Oleg Lobov, another close Yeltsin aide, was formerly the chairman of the executive committee of the Sverdlovsk oblast council. Gennadii Burbulis, the former first deputy prime minister, was also from Sverdlovsk but did not come from the former local CPSU leadership.[11] These Sverdlovsk comrades were balanced by another set of advisers close to Yelstin, including Yurii Skokov, head of the newly created Security Council; Lev Sukhanov, Yeltsin's former first assistant at the Ministry of Construction; Mikhail Poltoranin, former deputy prime minister; and Yurii Boldyrev, the former general inspector of the Russian Federation.

These associates in Yeltsin's inner circle have acted as a buffer between Yeltsin and the rest of both the government and the presidential apparat. Many people's deputies as well as officials in Yeltsin's own government have complained that this "mafia" has censored information received by the president, limited access to him, and drafted most of his presidential decrees. Critics have charged that they have sought to preserve the interest of the old *nomenklatura* at the expense of genuine market and democratic reform.[12] After a series of setbacks to the president's agenda during and after the Seventh Congress of People's Deputies in December 1993, several key Yeltsin advisers, including Burbulis, Poltoranin, Petrov, and Boldyrev, were removed or reassigned. Yeltsin's new chief of staff, Sergei Filatov, has incorporated several Democratic Russia leaders into the presidential staff as a means of improving cooperation and communication between Yeltsin and Russia's democratic forces.

The most significant new executive institution may be the Russian Security Council.[13] On July 7, 1992, Yeltsin signed a decree granting the Security Council the authority to review, oversee, and coordinate the administration of all government actions.[14] Yeltsin appointed a former manager of a Moscow-based arms manufacturing firm, Yurii Skokov, as the first head of this new, all-powerful institution and invited only key government officials to serve on the council.[15] In addition to Yeltsin and Skokov, members include Vice President Rutskoi; parliamentary speaker Ruslan Khasbulatov and, until his appointment as chief of staff, Khasbulatov's first deputy, Sergei Filatov; the heads of the KGB, defense, and internal affairs; and, most recently, Sergei Shakhrai. Like the old CPSU Politburo, this extraordinary government body potentially could assume unlimited powers beyond the control of the parliament or any other political authority. Thus far, however, it has not moved to assume this role.

The Congress of People's Deputies

In the immediate aftermath of the coup, Russia's parliament eagerly gave President Yeltsin a mandate to establish political authority by granting the president the power to rule by decree. Growing concern over the form and structure of the executive branch, however, prompted major challenges to Yeltsin's government during the Sixth Congress of People's Deputies in April 1992, the Seventh Congress in December 1992, and the extraordinary session of the Congress in March 1993. The final division of power between the executive and legislative branches of government has yet to be determined.

During the prelude to the Sixth Congress, it appeared that the president and the Presidium of the Supreme Soviet had reached a compromise whereby Yeltsin agreed to incorporate more "industrialists" into his government and provide additional subsidies for state enterprises in return for a vote of confidence for his government and the extension of the extraordinary powers the parliament had granted him in the fall. All bets were off, however, after Congress Chairman Ruslan Khasbulatov publicly chastised Yeltsin's government and unexpectedly proposed a resolution that would have stripped the government of its extraordinary powers and required the naming of a new prime minister within three months. The resolution also provided for greater social welfare restitutions and new subsidies to state-owned enterprises, two acts that Gaidar vehemently opposed. During the Congress, Khasbulatov had also publicly ridiculed the "children in pink shorts" (the Russian government) for threatening to resign, claiming that the Congress would not be blackmailed by anybody. Upon being called "children," all of Yeltsin's ministers walked out of the Congress. Infuriated by Khasbulatov's resolution and behavior, the entire Yeltsin government submitted their resignations to the president the following day.

Khasbulatov backed down two days later; the Congress passed a resolution by an overwhelming majority that supported Yeltsin's government and his reform package. Soon after, however, Yeltsin appointed to his government three new deputy prime ministers closely associated with the industrial lobby—Vladimir Shumeiko, Georgii Khizha, and Viktor Chernomyrdin. Although Yeltsin later named Yegor Gaidar to replace himself as acting prime minister, the appointment of the new deputy prime ministers was a major concession to the parliament.[16]

The Seventh Congress, held in December 1992, launched an even more serious attack against Yeltsin's executive power. The Congress failed by a narrow margin to approve a set of constitutional amendments that would have empowered the parliament to approve and dismiss all government ministers. The Congress did, however, remove the president's power to rule by decree and rejected Yeltsin's first choice for prime minister, Yegor Gaidar, who heretofore had served as acting prime minister. After initially threatening to hold a referendum on the disbanding of the

Congress, Yeltsin capitulated to the conservative parliament by nominating Viktor Chernomyrdin, a former oil and gas minister in the Gorbachev government, to be the new prime minister. One close observer of Russian politics called the rejection of Gaidar Yeltsin's "most serious political setback since coming to power 18 months ago."[17] Without any change in the composition or constitution of Russia's state institutions, power had shifted away from the executive and back to the Congress of People's Deputies.

The gravest assault by the Congress on presidential power mobilized in March 1993 during an extraordinary session convened to discuss the planned referendum on a new Russian constitution. Fearing a presidential victory in the vote, the Congress voted to cancel the referendum and moved to strip the executive office of even further powers. After the close of the Congress, Yeltsin rebutted by temporarily suspending its powers until a plebiscite in April on confidence in the president, a new constitution, and a new electoral law. In response, the Congress reassembled with the intention of impeaching the president. After several attempts at compromise, including a mutual commitment by both the president and the chairman of the Congress, Ruslan Khasbulatov, to hold elections for both the presidency and the parliament, the Congress nonetheless took a vote on impeachment. The motion failed by a narrow margin. The crisis, however, confused even further the balance and division of powers between the executive and legislative branches of government.

The peculiar composition of the current Russian parliament in itself impedes stabilization of the balance between executive and legislative power. The Congress of People's Deputies was elected to office in the spring of 1990, before the collapse of communism, before the formation of political parties, and before the creation of a Russian presidency. At the time, compared to the Union-level Congress of People's Deputies, this organ appeared progressive; although it took three ballots, this body did elect Boris Yeltsin as its chairman that spring. In the context of the current political spectrum, however, the Congress and the Supreme Soviet have come to represent the last bastion of conservative forces. Most important, the parliament has not reached a consensus about the basic system of government and economy needed for Russia. Conservatives, liberals, communists, and fascists all are represented in this one chamber. The absence of a common denominator has fueled polarization and impeded the formalization of democratic procedures for resolving issues before the parliament.

Although alignments within the parliament are constantly in flux, three main parliamentary blocs crystallized during the events surrounding the Sixth Congress of People's Deputies. These blocs have remained in place, although with varying degrees of support, through the subsequent crises in December 1992 and March 1993. Supporters of Yeltsin and his government's reforms constitute one bloc. This loose coalition, called the "Coalition in Support of Reforms," originally included the Democratic Russia faction, *Gruppa Reforma* (Reform Group), the "radical democrats," the Social Democratic-Republican faction, and the People's Party for a Free Russia. During the Sixth Congress of People's Deputies, this constellation of forces, supported by the quickly created Citizens' Society, rallied in support of Gaidar and the rest of Yeltsin's government. During the Seventh Congress, however, the People's Party for a Free Russia quit the coalition and several individual members also defected, leaving within the Congress fewer than 200 deputies who firmly supported Yeltsin.

The second bloc within the parliament is the conservative one, known as *Rossiiskoe Edinstvo* (Russian Unity). This coalition unites former Communists such as Boris Tarasov of *Otchizna* (Fatherland) and Ivan Rybkin (Communists of Russia), newly emerging nationalist leaders such as Viktor Aksiuchits and Mikhail Astafiev of *Rossiiskii Soyuz* (Russian Union), and nationalist-Communists such as Vladimir Isakov and Sergei Baburin of *Rossiya* (Russia).[18] Formed on the eve of the Sixth Congress, this conservative coalition has severely criticized Gaidar and his reforms, asserting that his economists are puppets of Western capitalism bent on destroying Russia's economic potential. Upon Gaidar's removal at the Seventh Congress, this coalition vowed to topple Yeltsin next, a task in which they almost succeeded in March.

Between these two extremes are a handful of independent factions that have become increasingly critical of Yeltsin's government. Some, such as the *Promyshlennyi Soyuz* (Industrial Union), represent specific social groups formed during the

Communist era and therefore have tended to side with the conservative coalition on most issues. Others, such as *Smena* (New Generation), agitate for the further strengthening of parliamentary powers. Consequently, they increasingly have sided against the "democratic" coalition in reaction to the mistakes and pursuits of power by Yeltsin's executive.[19]

Judiciary Power

In January 1992, the Supreme Soviet nominated 11 judges to sit on Russia's first Constitutional Court. Two more judges were added later. Although the court still had no new constitution to defend, Yeltsin, in concert with Russian parliamentarians, decided to create the court anyway as a first step toward creating an independent judiciary.

As a new institution, the court has yet to fix its place within the balance of power in the new Russian government. The court's initial decisions demonstrated its potential as a third force in Russia's new political life. The court's first major decision, on January 14, 1992, was to annul a presidential decree that merged the KGB (Committee on State Security) and the MVD (Ministry of Internal Affairs) into one institution. Although Yeltsin's legal adviser Sergei Shakhrai initially criticized the court's decision as a political rather than a legal one, the Yeltsin government eventually abided by the judgment of the court and appointed separate ministers for both institutions.

The court's second major decision was not so successful. In March 1992, several Russian people's deputies pressed the court to judge the constitutionality of Tatarstan's referendum on independence. In haste, the court ruled that the referendum was unconstitutional. Tatarstan ignored the court's decision and held the referendum. By appearing to act under political pressure, the court undermined its legitimacy as an independent third force. Because it was unable to enforce its decision, the court exposed the weakness and lack of authority of this new institution.

Starting in the summer of 1992, the court was given the unprecedented responsibility of reviewing the legality of the Communist Party of the Soviet Union, when former CPSU members petitioned the court to review President Yeltsin's decree banning the party in August 1991. Yeltsin's team responded by peti-

tioning the court to review the constitutionality of actions undertaken by the CPSU over the last 70 years. The overtly political
content of this case raised doubts as to whether the court will be
able to establish its independent authority irrespective of current
politics. Communists on trial as well as some "democratic"
deputies in the Russian parliament have even accused the court of
working as a prosecutor's office for Yeltsin's government. The
court ultimately upheld the president's ban but refused to judge
the entire 70-year history of the Communist Party.

After its measured decision on the legality of the CPSU, the
court began to act as a third force of last resort turned to by individuals and political movements of all ideological orientations during
toward the end of 1992. Nationalists turned to the court to ask for a
ruling on whether the president's ban on the National Salvation
Front (discussed in the following chapter) was constitutional. The
court ruled it was not. In a similar manner, the radical-democrat
faction of the Congress of People's Deputies appealed to the court
to rule on the parliamentary resolution on price controls.[20] Most
dramatically, however, both Yeltsin and the Congress invited Valerii
Zorkin, the chief justice of the court, to mediate a compromise
agreement between the executive and legislative branches of government regarding the selection of a prime minister at the Seventh
Congress. At that moment, the court appeared to have arrived as
an independent, neutral force in Russian politics.

Two months later, however, Zorkin discredited the institution,
first by openly siding with Ruslan Khasbulatov rather than the
president on holding a referendum and, second, by declaring a
presidential decree unconstitutional before having even read it.
This last act prompted Ernest Ametistov, another justice on the
Constitutional Court, to consider charges of unconstitutional
behavior against Zorkin himself. The entire series of events seriously undermined the legitimacy of this new institution and will
impede respect for the rule of law more generally at every level of
government.

A New Russian Constitution?

A central obstacle to defining the divisions of state power is the
absence of a post-Communist constitution. Russia has not completed the constitution-making process, "one of the major activi-

ties of a transition to democracy," nor has it adopted a temporary set of "rules of the game" for government until a new constitution has been approved. Instead, Russia has relied on the 1977 Constitution of the USSR, the work of Leonid Brezhnev. This document has been amended more than 300 times in the last years by the Congress of People's Deputies, making it internally inconsistent, confusing, and illegitimate for most Russian citizens.[21]

The first official draft constitution, the "Rumyantsev" version, guaranteed the primacy of the Supreme Soviet over the presidency by granting the legislative organ the power to recall the "government" (i.e., the prime minister and his cabinet).[22] Fearful of a conservative congress blocking radical reforms, Anatolii Sobchak proposed an alternative constitutional draft that gave the presidential office more autonomy from the parliament. Yeltsin, although formally the chairman of the Constitutional Commission of the Supreme Soviet, did not support his own commission's draft during the Sixth Congress. Instead, his adviser, Sergei Shakhrai, drafted yet another "presidential" constitution that further strengthened the powers of the president via-à-vis the parliament. The Congress's debate on the constitution ended in stalemate, with Brezhnev's 1977 constitution, albeit amended, remaining in force.

In July 1992, Oleg Rumyantsev convinced Yeltsin to reassume the chair on the Constitutional Commission. Yeltsin then secured approval from the Congress of People's Deputies to hold a referendum on the basic principles of the constitution, scheduled for April 1993.[23] The latest constitutional draft is an amended version of the Rumyantsev draft that gives the presidential office greater power than before. In this version, the Congress of People's Deputies and the Supreme Soviet are collapsed into one smaller, bicameral legislature. The parliament gains the right to review candidates for prime minister and for internal, foreign, defense, and security ministers, but it does not have the power to remove the president. The parliament would retain the right to legislate, but the executive would assume general responsibility for economic matters. The right to private property will be guaranteed in the constitution. At a minimum, the adoption of this constitution would establish a starting point for developing the delicate balances of power between the Russian executive, legislative, and judicial branches of power. Until such a new constitution is adopted and respected, however, Russia will continue to endure periodic and destabilizing crises of state power.

Defining the Government: The Division of Vertical Power

Local Executive-Legislative Feuds

Yeltsin attempted to replicate the centrality of the executive at the national level at lower levels of government while at the same time divesting local councils of the little power and authority they had gained after the spring 1990 elections. As noted above, Yeltsin created the new position of *glavy administratsii* (head of administration) at the oblast, city, and district levels. At the oblast level, these "governors" effectively replaced the chairman of the Executive Committee of the oblast council (*ispolkom*) as the new local executive, reporting directly to the national government rather than to the oblast council.[24] These governors then named new mayors and regional heads of administration in their oblasts.

As institutions, these new executives were a revolutionary departure from the old system. The people who initially assumed these offices, however, were often former first secretaries of the CPSU: a legacy of Russia's peaceful revolution.[25] Even in Nizhni Novgorod, where Boris Nemtsov from Democratic Russia was named governor, the vast majority of the executive apparat had formerly worked in the local committee of the Communist Party or the *ispolkom* of the oblast council.[26]

To fortify executive authority (subordinate to Moscow) over local councils, Yeltsin added a second institution—the "presidential representative"—to parallel these heads of administration. Initially, Yeltsin appointed experienced administrators as heads of administration and people close to himself as local presidential representatives. He hoped that these presidential emissaries would shadow local heads of administration until the elections scheduled for December 1991. By then, these presidential representatives were to have developed the necessary skills to govern locally. They then would run for head of administration in the December elections and replace the old *nomenklatura* leaders.

When Yeltsin decided that elections in December were too risky, however, the presidential representatives were assigned new responsibilities, including the most important one of oversight and implementation of presidential decrees at the local level. Informally, they also review all major appointments in the local government administration. Local officials have referred to these people as Yeltsin's commissars.

Local activists from Democratic Russia and other democratically oriented parties and organizations have sharply criticized these new institutions and the people who fill them. Not only are those who hold the new positions former Communist functionaries rather than leaders of democratic groups, but with the exception of Moscow and St. Petersburg, these new executives were appointed rather than elected. Even advocates of more executive authority such as Anatolii Sobchak have complained about the new structure and Yeltsin's choices in filling it:

> The choice of people and a certain policy in forming structures are simply not acceptable to me. I think this is the sphere in which the most serious mistakes are being made today. As a specialist, I can see that there is no viable administrative structure. Duplicate and parallel apparatuses are being formed—the president's administration and the government with undifferentiated and ill-defined functions. There are very few new people.[27]

Other critics also have accused Yeltsin of replicating the dual system of power practiced by the CPSU.[28] In their own defense, Yeltsin's team has argued that Russia needs a strong executive staffed by competent administrators to execute radical economic reform. As the "democrats" lack such skills, Yeltsin has turned to Russia's most experienced bureaucrats—functionaries from the CPSU.

In the shadow of these new executive institutions, local city councils have been reduced to simply reviewing government actions rather than initiating legislation. In cities where "democrats" once formed a majority, divisions between the mayor's office and the city council have hindered if not paralyzed effective government. The Moscow City Council, for instance, has repeatedly attempted to nullify executive decisions regarding privatization, ministerial appointments, and taxation. Exhausted with battling his former allies in the city council, Popov finally resigned in June 1992.[29] After having pressed for Popov's resignation, local legislators then refused to recognize his successor, Yurii Luzhkov. Instead, the city council called for the election of a new mayor.

The conflict between Moscow's executive and city council is reproduced in many other Russian cities. The relative success of the capital's council blocking the executive policy, however, is the exception, not the rule. In the vast majority of other cities and oblasts in which "democrats" managed a weak minority position within the council, power has shifted to the local executives.

Decentralization

The executive structure decreed into existence by Yeltsin has retarded the process of decentralization even in those few oblasts where Yeltsin loyalists serve. In Russian oblasts, economic collapse—not nationalist or religious renewal—has been the main stimulus of political decentralization. Forced to fare on their own, many oblast governors have moved to keep local resources and production within their territory by passing special decrees declaring that local laws supersede federal laws. Ownership of natural resources has been claimed in Komi, Tatarstan, Yenisei Republic (Krasnoyarsk) and several other Siberian localities. Custom posts now regulate trade between several oblasts, while tax rates, the method of privatization, and the percentage of revenues paid to the center now vary widely from region to region. By the summer of 1992, analysts counted more than 40 regions located within the Russian Federation that had ceased to send monies into the federal budget.[30] Some regions even have entertained issuing their own currency simply because the money supply from Moscow has fallen so far behind wages owed to workers. In many regions of Russia, state employees (i.e., the vast majority of the working population) go several months without being paid simply because there is no local cash. Large local factories also have begun to print their own monetary instruments.[31]

The paralysis of federal power catalyzed by stalemates between the Congress and the president has prodded regional leaders to assume even greater responsibility for the local economy and government. After the government crisis in March 1993, dozens of local leaders even called for the creation of a "federal council" to act as an alternative government structure dedicated to the needs of Russia's regions. It is uncertain when and at what level this devolution of power will end.

Conclusion

In seeking to destroy Communist rule, Russia's "democrats" unleashed anarchic forces. In seeking to arrest anarchy and impede further disintegration, Russia's "democrats" have tried to construct a soft authoritarian state. The project of consolidating a democratic polity, complete with established procedures and due process, has been postponed. Many leaders of the Communist opposition have argued that this *peredyshka* (respite) from democracy is a necessary condition during the transition to a market economy. State Councillor Sergei Stankevich, for instance, has argued that

> at all times, in all countries, intensive reform efforts were implemented only by leaders who were somewhat authoritarian. . . . Never and nowhere has a transition of society to a qualitatively new state been accomplished during . . . a flourishing parliamentary democracy.[32]

Even more bluntly, radicals within Democratic Russia called for the dissolution of the parliament and local councils altogether.

Are there alternatives? Perhaps, as Stankevich has argued, Russia's economic revolution requires an iron-handed state to succeed.[33] As Adam Przeworksi has succinctly stated,

> reforms tend to be enacted by fiat, or railroaded through legislatures without any changes reflecting the divergence of opinions. The political style of implementation tends toward rule by decree; governments seek to mobilize their supporters rather than accept the compromises that might result from public consultation. In the end, the society is taught that it can vote but not choose; legislatures are given the impression that they have no role to play in the elaboration of policy; nascent political parties, trade

unions, and other organizations learn that their voices do not count. The autocratic character of such "Washington-style" reforms helps to undermine representative institutions, personalize politics, and engender a climate in which politics become either reduced to fixes, or else inflated in search of redemption. Thus even when neoliberal reforms make economic sense, they weaken representative institutions.[34]

Reforms accomplished by fiat quickly lose legitimacy, however. If resisted by the majority, or even a vocal minority, they must often be implemented by coercion and force.[35] Additionally, the Russian state still owns more than 90 percent of property and productive resources. Without democratic mechanisms for societal control in place, this state can quickly become omnipotent once again.

Finally, the theoretical rationale for establishing a mild authoritarian regime must come to grips with the political and economic realities of Russia's collapsing state. Russia's republics have acquired tremendous local autonomy, while many of Russia's oblasts ignore Moscow's directives. Similarly, Russia is on the verge of massive privatization. Once local bureaucrats become owners, they will have little incentive to resubmit to some government authority. Given this extensive decentralization of power, a move from the center toward greater control could trigger militant resistance. The last attempt to restore central authority in August 1991 precipitated the dissolution of the Soviet Union. A similar move now could unravel the Russian Federation.

5
Russia's Post-Communist Political Parties and Social Movements

During the months of polarization leading up to the August 1991 coup, democracy and (to a lesser extent) the market were "ideologies of opposition" adopted by revolutionary forces to mobilize anti-Communist sentiment into a cohesive social movement. As discussed in chapter 3, these ideas proved more effective at mobilizing social forces against the ancien régime than did neocommunism, nationalism, or socialist democracy.

The simplified poles of "Communist" and "democrat" evaporated after August 1991. With the straitjacket of this dichotomy removed, Russia's post-Communist politics has begun to develop along new trajectories. Some parties and social movements that were very active during liberalized communism now play no role in the post-Communist era, while other parties and social groups born prematurely in the Communist era are emerging as real forces. For instance, the Democratic Union, the first non-Communist political party in the Soviet Union and an instrumental catalyst for early anti-Communist social formations, has become marginalized in Russia's nascent post-Communist civil society.[1] At the other end of the spectrum, professional organizations such as the Party for Economic Freedom played virtually no role in the revolutionary transition but may have a significant future once capitalism and/or pluralism take hold. Viktor Aksiuchits, for instance, claims that his Russian Christian Democratic Movement (RCDM) is a party of the future. As he explained, "Given the crisis in the country, it is hard to distinguish the RCDM's social basis. Such parties as the RCDM fare well only in a stable political situation."[2]

In between the past and the future are two other kinds of social interest groups and parties: those based on new social forces defined within the context of Russia's transitional political and economic order and those based on social groups constructed under communism that have adjusted (or have the potential to retool) to the new socioeconomic order. Most important, a vast existing social base of industrial and agricultural workers could be mobilized by some political party or movement. Although groups such at Yurii Chernechenko's Peasants' Party, the Union of Workers' Collectives, the former Communist trade unions, and a dozen neo-Communist parties already claim to represent the interests of these groups, none of them truly does.[3] Whether these social forces are temporarily dormant or are undergoing a more permanent redefinition, requiring correspondingly new kinds of parties and unions to represent their interests, is still unclear. These ambiguities surrounding Russia's unfolding civil society complicate and inhibit democratic consolidation.

The Demise of Russia's Democratic Opposition

Not only personal rivalries but real ideological differences began to distinguish parties, movements, and factions from each other in the spring of 1991. This process of differentiation accelerated after the putsch. Without a common enemy, the united front forged under the banner of Democratic Russia collapsed. In November 1991 at the Second Congress of Democratic Russia, the *Narodnoe Soglasie* (People's Accord) bloc—consisting of the Democratic Party of Russia (Nikolai Travkin), the Russian Christian Democratic Movement (Viktor Aksiuchits), and the Constitutional Democratic Party—the Party of People's Freedom (Mikhail Astafiev)—quit the coalition for good. In February 1992, a major battle erupted within the movement when two of the cochairmen elected at the November Congress, Yurii Afanasiev and Marina Salye, did not receive enough votes to become members of the Council of Representatives. Claiming voter fraud, these two and their allies have tried to organize an extraordinary Democratic Russia Congress to redetermine the leadership of the movement.[4] Finally, the Republican Party of Russia and the Social Democratic Party of Russia, although nominally still members of the coalition, began to distance their organizations from the increasingly radical tactics of the Democratic Russia Movement.

In addition to Democratic Russia, virtually every major political party suffered post-putsch divisions and splits. Within the Democratic Party, Aleksandr Sungurov formed the "liberal faction" to oppose Travkin's nationalist proclivities. The Russian Christian Democratic Movement's Father Gleb Yakunin resigned to protest Viktor Aksiuchits's embrace of the Russian nationalists. Although less developed, rival factions also have formed around leadership clashes in the Republican Party, the Social Democratic Party, and the People's Party for a Free Russia.[5]

At the same time, factions within the Communist Party, formed under Gorbachev but still united within the CPSU organization until August 1991, have now founded several dozen new political parties, fronts, and factions. Several months before the putsch, the liberal wing of the CPSU, headed by Eduard Shevardnadze and Aleksandr Yakovlev, had already drafted initial plans for the creation of a new party that, like the Democratic Platform, aspired to unite progressive Communists still in the CPSU with prominent politicians already outside of Communist Party structures. In December 1991, their Movement for Democratic Reform held its founding congress.[6] The parliamentary faction, Communists for Democracy, headed by Aleksandr Rutskoi, also emerged from the CPSU to form the People's Party for a Free Russia. Dozens of new Communist-oriented parties and fronts sprouted from the conservative wing of the CPSU after the party was banned in August 1991.

Additionally, nationalist and patriotic groups, which were on the fringes of political activity between 1988 and 1991, have reinvigorated their activities after the collapse of the Soviet Union. Closet nationalists from both democratic and Communist camps have joined their cause.

Finally, a whole set of new actors has appeared as a result of Russia's new post-Communist socioeconomic conditions. Associations of entrepreneurs, independent trade unions, and industrial lobbies have emerged to defend and represent a new set of interests created by Russia's attempt at rapid transition to a market economy.

Reconsolidation

The period of dissolution, fragmentation, and articulation of new political movements, parties, and organizations initiated by the August putsch lasted almost a year. By the end of the summer of 1992, a new period of consolidation of political forces began in response to Russia's new political and economic situation. Although it is difficult to delineate absolute cleavages, three major political alliances have emerged: the Coalition in Support of Reforms, Civic Union, and the nationalist-Communist front. Superimposing Western notions of left and right or liberal and conservative often distorts rather than clarifies Russia's constellation of political forces. Instead of being drawn linearly from left to right, the Russian political map must be charted along several different axes. Three variables that help to plot Russia's parties and movements are (1) attitude toward market reforms and the Yeltsin government, (2) attitude toward state organization and power, and (3) methods used to realize these objectives. Although even these distinctions are not always clear, they help to describe the principal cleavages among the three major political groupings in post-Communist Russia.

Democratic Russia Reincarnated

Although weakened by splits at the top, the surviving remnants of Democratic Russia still represent one of the most critical forces in post-Communist Russia. After surviving two major splits in the fall of 1991 and the winter of 1992, the leadership of the former coalition initiated a strategy to reunite all democratic forces still supportive of Yeltsin's reforms. The Sixth Congress of People's Deputies, held in April 1992, provided the first major stimulus for reconsolidation, as Yeltsin's government had to be defended against a conservative challenge.[7] The second major stimulus came from the streets during the summer of 1992, when a loose alliance of nationalists and Communists —the "red-brown" coalition—launched a series of protests outside the Russian television station Ostankino to demand television access. In response, Democratic Russia organized an antifascist rally at the television station, its first public demonstration since the putsch. Finally, on July 4–5, 1992, Democratic Russia in conjunction with several other organizations and several leading personalities, convened the Forum of Democratic Forces. In addition to Democratic Russia and its affiliates, participants at this meeting included Yegor Gaidar, Anatolii Chubais, Andrei Nechayev, Andrei Kozyrev, Gennadii Burbulis, Gavriil Popov, and Galina Staravoitova. This forum, later renamed *Demokraticheskii Vybor* (Democratic

Choice), aimed to consolidate Russia's "democratic" forces and thereby reinvigorate popular support for liberal economic reforms.

Economic policy. Democratic Russia, and its most recent incarnation, Democratic Choice, have supported the Gaidar strategy of free prices, unregulated markets, and rapid and comprehensive privatization. To support this agenda, Democratic Russia created the Social Committees for Russian Reform in December 1991. Officially, these committees have been created on the basis of Yeltsin's campaign cells (during the 1991 election) and thus are independent of Democratic Russia, although in many cities the vast majority of the Committees' organizers are members of Democratic Russia.[8] This network has established local organizations throughout Russia to advise people and enterprises about market reforms, especially privatization.[9] The Committees also have worked closely with the Supreme Soviet's Committee on Economic Reform (chaired by Democratic Russia activist Pyotr Phillipov) to draft a new set of regulations on privatization, approved in June 1992.[10] In addition, the Committees have begun to monitor the work of Yeltsin's local heads of administration, reporting on those who are inhibiting reform.

Besides the activities of the Committees, Democratic Russia factions in councils at all levels have rallied in support of radical economic reform. Most important, the Democratic Russia faction in the Russian Congress of People's Deputies organized the coalition that prevented the derailment of Gaidar's reform package at the Sixth Congress. The coalition showed signs of attrition, however, at the Seventh Congress in December 1992 at which the Democratic Russia bloc could not deliver enough votes to approve Gaidar as prime minister. And during the vote on impeachment conducted by the Congress of People's Deputies in March 1993, only 267 deputies voted for preserving Yeltsin.[11]

Different groups within Democratic Russia support Yeltsin and his market reforms to varying degrees. The radical wing of the movement, led by Yurii Afanasiev and Leonid Batkin, have all but quit their activity in Democratic Russia because of their dissatisfaction with Yeltsin. The self-proclaimed "pragmatists" within Democratic Russia also have criticized the process of Yeltsin's economic reform but consider the Yeltsin-Gaidar strategy the only possible path for Russia today.

Moreover, Democratic Russia's support for Yeltsin's economic reform is not based on the concrete interests of Democratic Russia activists. Although anyone, in theory, might gain from a market economy, the real winners in the short term—the new entrepreneurs—are no longer affiliated with Democratic Russia. The movement's activists are mostly academics and white-collar bureaucrats, who are most threatened, at least in the near future, by market reforms. Democratic Russia's support for radical reform stems as much from the organization's identification with Yeltsin as it does from any rational assessment of concrete interests. In opposition, Democratic Russia always stood behind Yeltsin, even when Yeltsin himself distanced himself from the social movement.[12] Now that Yeltsin is in power, Democratic Russia's leaders believe that they must fully support the new government through this difficult transition period, even if their interests do not always coincide.[13] In addition, vehement anti-Communist sentiment continues to activate Democratic Russia loyalists even when their own individual interests are not served by the immediate consequences of Yeltsin's economic reform.

The state. On the question of state power, Democratic Russia and its most recent manifestation, Democratic Choice, have adopted a decidedly quiet position. When the Soviet Union existed, Democratic Russia championed national self-determination for all republics. Initially after the putsch, several Democratic Russia leaders also bestowed upon autonomous republics within the Russian Federation the right to secede, if done by democratic means. Yurii Afanasiev, for example, said of the Russian Federation

> in my view, Russia should be united, but not indivisible. The national territories—such as Tatarstan, Yakutia, the Ural region, the northern Caucasus, and so on—must have independence, autonomy, their own laws, parliaments, taxes—call them what you will. If not—the country will explode in bloodshed.[14]

As this issue has become increasingly controversial, however, the movement as a whole has drawn back from Afanasiev's drastic position. Moreover, many of those who support a weak federal system have left Democratic Russia. Democratic Russia leaders have even initiated a new set of dialogues with democratic forces in other new states of the former Soviet Union with the aim of creating a new institution similar to the European parliament.

Tactics. Democratic Russia's success during the Soviet period resulted from its ability to organize massive political meetings on the streets in opposition to the Communist regime. Rather than seeking compromise or accommodation, Democratic Russia has continued to use confrontational and aggressive tactics against its opponents. For instance, many within Democratic Russia have called for full disclosure of all present government officials who were ever affiliated with the KGB. In response to the Russian parliament's inability to adopt a new constitution, Democratic Russia initiated a campaign to adopt a new constitution through a referendum. Democratic Russia also threatened to use the referendum weapon to dissolve the parliament and institute a new law on land ownership. Mass populist actions, such as electoral campaigns, street rallies, and petition drives, are Democratic Russia's most successful means of political action.

Allies. The July 4 meeting of the Forum of Democratic Forces, or Democratic Choice, clarified who supported whom. To the surprise even of the event's organizers, almost all of the political parties and organizations from the old Democratic Russia coalition, with the exception of *Narodnoe Soglasie* members (the Democratic Party of Russia, the Russian Christian Democratic Movement, and Mikhail Astafiev's Constitutional Democratic Party), attended and participated in some capacity. Likewise, most members of the parliamentary faction *Gruppa Reform* played an active role in both organizing the meeting and setting the agenda. The People's Party for a Free Russia (Rutskoi's Party), never a member of Democratic Russia, sent observers. Finally, the majority of Yeltsin's senior government officials at that time, including Yegor Gaidar, Gennadii Burbulis, Anatoly Chubais, Andrei Kozyrev, and Andrei Nechayev, attended the meeting, delivering their ringing endorsement and support for the formation of a new, all-powerful political movement to promote radical reform.

In November 1992, in a further move to consolidate the democratic flank, President Yeltsin rekindled the idea of forming a presidential party. The idea first arose in February 1991 when Democratic Russia asked Yeltsin to join the movement as a means of consolidating Russia's democratic forces.[15] Yeltsin refused, not wanting to limit his base of support to only "democrats," but the idea lingered. During the June 1991 presidential election, Yeltsin's campaign manager, Gennadii Burbulis, erected the skeletal structure for a presidential party by appointing 100 famous Yeltsin loyalists (*dovernie litsa*) to organize and coordinate campaign cells throughout Russia.[16] These cells, independent of the Democratic Russia campaign for Yeltsin, were then to serve as the nuclei for a new presidential party. The August coup, however, created the imperative of governing, not party building. As a result, many of Yeltsin's trusted colleagues from the June campaign were named local executives—*glavy administratsii* or heads of administration—in oblasts and cities in Russia. The recent creation of associations of both governors and other heads of administration, coupled with Yeltsin's appointment of Burbulis as his deputy for creating a new party, suggests that a new presidential party still may coalesce.

Despite these prospects, the "democratic" banner no longer represents a coalition of political parties and organizations. Democratic Choice leaders increasingly have acted as an independent political party, alienating other parties and movements. Most of Democratic Russia's Moscow leaders belong to no political party or affiliation other than Democratic Russia. This is not the case in the provinces, however, because many Democratic Russia local cells were formed as coalitions of local political parties, especially the Democratic Party of Russia. Therefore, the Moscow initiative to create a Democratic Russia party has created problems of allegiance in small towns throughout Russia.

Unwilling to subordinate their autonomy, most political parties of a democratic orientation in both the center and the periphery have begun to distance themselves from Democratic Russia and its leadership in particular. For instance, the Russian Movement for Democratic Reform, founded by Gavriil Popov, an original cochair of Democratic Russia, refused to sign a joint statement issued after the July 1992 conference for fear of being too closely associated with Democratic Russia. Individual members of the Social Democratic Party of Russia (SDPR) joined this new coalition, but the party did not. Instead, the SDPR has joined the People's Party of Russia (Telman Gdlyan), the Social Liberal

Association, (Vladimir Filin), the Peasants' Party of Russia (Yurii Chernechenko), and the Young Russia Union, in creating an alternative coalition of parties called *Novaya Rossiya* (New Russia). Leaders of *Novaya Rossiya* hope to create a third choice for voters and political activists, in addition to Democratic Russia and the newly emerging right wing. The "democratic" flank of Russia's new political spectrum can rally when called upon and may even reunite under Yeltsin's leadership, but the depth of unity within this bloc has dwindled significantly since the August coup.

Prospects. The organizational structure and modus operandi of Democratic Russia and its new incarnation, the Coalition in Support of Reforms (*Demokraticheskii Vybor* or Democratic Choice), have not adapted effectively to the new political situation in Russia. Democratic Russia's major asset has always been its grass-roots organizational reach into every major city and town throughout the Russian Federation. Although this organizational structure has eroded, at least temporarily, since the coup, the Social Committees for Russian Reform, created and operated by local Democratic Russia activists, have maintained a nominal level of political mobilization at the local level. The increasing ascendancy of local politics and their corresponding political organizations and movements have accorded to the Social Committees for Russian Reform concrete and sustaining tasks that, in turn, serve to support this political network.

Mass mobilization, however, is not the most effective technique for influencing current government policy. When a clearly identifiable enemy existed during the Soviet period, Democratic Russia masterfully constructed a mass movement based on an anti-Communist, antistate, and antipolitics ideology. In the post-Communist Russian era, however, Democratic Russia has supported Yeltsin's government without being directly involved in the formation of government policy. Earlier, Democratic Russia drew on grass-roots support from below to confront, and ultimately dethrone, the Soviet government above; since the collapse of the Soviet Union, the movement has tried to persuade society to *support* from below government actions from above.

This reversal of roles has severely weakened Democratic Russia's effectiveness. At the grass-roots level, mobilization politics by a social movement in support of a government is much more difficult than fueling opposition to a hated regime. At the national government level, few Democratic Russia leaders serve in Yeltsin's government, while Democratic Russia's access to Yeltsin has decreased significantly.[17] Only the creation of a presidential party might save this political movement from complete disintegration.

Civic Union (*Grazhdanskii Soyuz*)

Civic Union and its affiliates constitute the second major social force to emerge in post-Communist Russian civil society. The impetus for this new movement originated with those political parties uncomfortable with Democratic Russia's radical tactics and fearful of a further weakening of the Russian state and economy. Nikolai Travkin, one of the founding leaders of this bloc, began searching for new allies who shared his commitment to a strong state after leaving Democratic Russia in November 1991. After a brief flirtation with the "red-brown" coalition of nationalists and Communists, Travkin eventually found a kindred spirit in Aleksandr Rutskoi, an outspoken critic of the proliferation of regional conflicts on Russia's borders and Gaidar's Western-oriented reform plan.[18] In March 1992, the Democratic Party of Russia signed a cooperation agreement with the People's Party for a Free Russia (Rutskoi's Party). Two months later, the Union of Industrialists and Entrepreneurs formed a political party, the All-Russian Union *Obnovlenie* (renewal), cochaired by Arkadii Volsky and Aleksandr Vladislavlev, in preparation for a political coalition with Travkin and Rutskoi.[19] These three parties then joined with the parliamentary faction *Smena* (new generation) to found Civic Union in June 1992.

The economy. Civic Union differs from Democratic Russia on all three issues outlined above. Regarding economic reform, Civic Union claims to support the creation of a market economy but rejects Gaidar's methods of achieving it. Members of Civic Union, especially Arkadii Volsky and Aleksandr Vladislavlev of *Obnovlenie*, first argued that the sequence of Gaidar's reforms was flawed: privatization should have been implemented first, price liberalization second. Now that this issue is no longer relevant, Civic Union seeks to change the method and pace of privatization, contending that, in the current economic environment, the voucher scheme will destroy Russia's industrial base.

Civic Union claims that the technology and procedure for distributing millions of vouchers will be difficult, corrupt, and slow in a country the size of Russia. It argues that in the interim between sorting out the voucher system and establishing real owners, the majority of Russian enterprises will go bankrupt through no fault of their own. In fact, Arkadii Volsky asserts that only about 10 percent of Russian enterprises are actually insolvent.

Leaders of Civic Union further claim that mass public privatization schemes through a voucher system will not redistribute ownership but will simply concentrate it in the hands of those who now have money: former black marketeers, the mafia, and foreigners.[20] These people will acquire vouchers and, eventually, stocks from common Russian citizens, gain controlling interests in Russia's most valuable properties, and then sell the assets of these enterprises for a quick profit without reference to the long-term interests of the individual firm. Because these "speculators" are not industrialists, they will not make the kind of investments needed to revitalize Russia's industrial base. Even if they were interested in preserving Russia's industrial capacity, they have neither the experience nor the training to run these industries effectively or efficiently. Therefore, Civic Union argues, directors and workers' collectives must have the first opportunity to become owners.[21] This kind of privatization requires a longer transition and therefore a continued role for the state in regulating and managing the Russian economy. During this longer transition period, Civic Union has argued, the government must own a controlling share of stock in all large joint stock companies, continue to subsidize these large industrial enterprises, provide long-term low interest rate loans for military enterprises undergoing conversion, eliminate inter-enterprise debt, and stimulate demand through wage and price indexing.[22]

The state. Unlike Democratic Russia, Civic Union has declared its unequivocal support for the creation of a strong, centralized state system. During his confrontations with Democratic Russia before the coup, Nikolai Travkin first propagated the notion of a "democratic *gosudarstvennik*," i.e., one who supports the maintenance of a strong, indivisible, but democratic state. At the time, Communists and nationalists had monopolized the concept, claiming that democrats were anti-Russian.[23] Travkin attempted to reclaim this patriotic discourse by arguing that only a strong state can protect the human rights of minorities against the tyranny of the majority.[24] He argued that democrats could still be supporters of the preservation of the Union and advocates of a strong state more generally.[25]

After the collapse of the Soviet Union, focus on maintaining a strong state shifted to the Russian level. Civic Union has argued that under no circumstances should autonomous republics be allowed to leave the Russian Federation. Vice President Rutskoi emphatically declared, "The breaking up of Russia is like death. And not only for us, but also for mankind. It is the death of the world."[26] The Democratic Party of Russia even urged the Sixth Congress of People's Deputies to resist Yeltsin's federal treaty because the agreement accorded de jure equal status to all signatories of the federation. Not surprisingly, this coalition has lobbied for the deployment of Russian soldiers abroad to defend Russians living in neighboring republics. Civic Union leaders have also supported petitions from neighboring territories that seek to join the Russian Federation.

Tactics. As for method, this coalition has called for the end of street demonstrations and the beginning of "constructive" engagement among all of Russia's main political forces. Since its inception, Civic Union has claimed to be in "constructive opposition" to Yeltsin's government, but not to Yeltsin himself. Arkadii Volsky has stated that President Yeltsin is the only stabilizing factor in Russia today. As a constructive opposition, Civic Union has preferred to operate behind the scenes rather than confronting opponents. Volsky's group in particular has functioned more as a lobby than as a political party, seeking back-room meetings with top government officials to influence changes in both the policy and the staff of Yeltsin's government. Unlike Democratic Russia, which is constantly struggling to raise money, financial supporters in the military industrial complex endow Civic Union with the means to operate as an effective political organization.

Allies. Civic Union has attracted several important allies, from both government and society. In addition to Vice President Rutskoi, a cofounder of the alliance, Deputy Prime Ministers Vladimir Shumeiko and Georgii Khizha have worked with Civic Union, while Prime Minister Viktor Chernomyrdin has closely identified with the Civic Union platform.[27] Sergei Gonchar', the chairman of the Moscow City Council, also participated in the founding congress, and Russian Supreme Soviet Chairman Ruslan Khasbulatov has made overtures toward the new coalition. Anatolii Sobchak, mayor of St. Petersburg, Sergei Stankevich, a presidential adviser, and Oleg Rumyantsev, the head of the Russian Constitutional Commission also have expressed their allegiances to this coalition. On the eve of the Seventh Congress of People's Deputies, in December 1992, Civic Union claimed to control more than 40 percent of all votes in the legislative body.

Because the Union of Industrialists and Entrepreneurs was a founding member through its political party, the All Russian Union *Obnovlenie*, Civic Union also claims the support of the vast majority of Russia's industrial managers. Russia's industrialists, however, are not a homogenous set of actors.[28] At various meetings of directors during the summer and fall of 1992, several directors criticized Arkadii Volsky, cochair of the All-Russian Union *Obnovlenie*, for misrepresenting their interests in the pursuit of his individual political career.[29] Moreover, at the November 1992 congress of the Russian Union of Industrialists and Entrepreneurs, only one-fourth of the delegates were actual enterprise directors. Despite these criticisms and the nascent formation of new industrial and director associations, Volsky's organization still enjoys the highest visibility.

Finally, even worker associations have entered into negotiations with this new political force. Both the Union of Workers' Collectives (STK), a group that claims to represent 3 million workers at large industrial enterprises, and the Federation of Independent Trade Unions, the former Communist trade union network, have become affiliated with the coalition.

Prospects. Civic Union has organized effectively to deal with Russia's post-Communist polity. The group has high-profile and popular leadership.[30] The individual actions of Volsky, Rutskoi, or Travkin can influence political debates within the Russian government.[31] As a result of their initial successes in promoting several of their allies into the highest ranks of Yeltsin's government, Civic Union has direct access to the highest of policymakers. Civic Union does not have representatives in every city and town as Democratic Russia does, but the kinds of activities this movement undertakes do not require grass-roots support.

Russia's highly volatile social structure, however, will severely challenge the continued viability of this political alliance. Civic Union has appealed to concrete social groups—directors, trade unions, and military officers—that formed under communism. As these groups are challenged and reorganized by Russia's post-Communist political economy, Civic Union will seek new bases of support; or it will assist these old class and social formations into making the transition; or it will attempt to freeze the transition and thereby maintain the hegemonic position of these social groups according to old, Communist methods of economic production and political administration.

As Russia's economy changes, particularly as a result of privatization, the apparent unanimity within these social groups dissipates. Already, Civic Union is competing with several new associations and federations to represent the "industrialists." As some directors become chief executive officers of profitable enterprises while others face bankruptcy or lose control of their factories, competing political organizations eventually will represent these different kinds of directors. The same will be true of different labor forces, which may divide and organize by industry, location, or even ethnic group. Given this highly volatile social structure, Civic Union may be only a temporary, albeit powerful, political alliance.

The "Reds" and the "Browns"

The third and most amorphous political force to emerge in post-Communist Russia is the "red-brown" coalition. Nationalism, a dormant ideology during the heyday of liberal politics in 1989 - 1991, has attracted new disciples from both the "Communist" and the "democratic" camps since the August coup. Communism, or neocommunism, has not mobilized the masses; but zealots espousing a Communist renaissance have been particularly vocal and visible in their campaigns, creating the image of a popular movement.

After several false starts, a large coalition of nationalist and Communist movements called the National Salvation Front formed in October 1992. Several days later, Yeltsin disbanded the Front, asserting that the group aimed to "fuel national dissent and pose a real threat to the integrity of the Russian Federation and the independence of neighboring sovereign states, in contravention of the fundamentals of the Russian constitutional system."[32] Front founders, however, ignored the decree and continued their activities, giving organization and unity to this third force in Russian politics.

The Front united behind two general issues: their hatred of Yeltsin and their nostalgia for the past. All consider Yeltsin and his government enemy number one, and all of the factions within the Front look longingly back into history for their conceptions of the ideal Russian or Soviet state. To which past Russia or the Soviet Union should return, however, is heatedly debated. Nina Andreeva's All-Union Communist Party of Bolsheviks, for instance, would like to return to the Stalinist era, while the Russian Communist Workers' Party has romanticized the Soviet era under Lenin. Meanwhile, groups such as Viktor Aksiuchits's Christian Democrats and Mikhail Astafiev's Kadets regard prerevolutionary Russia as the golden era. These assorted organizations wince at each other's ideological platforms. The level of their disdain for the current Russian government, however, has been sufficient to eclipse these tedious issues of whether Russia should return to communism or feudalism.

Not all nationalist or Communist groups joined the Front. In fact, several different tendencies can be identified within the red-brown bloc, of which only portions joined the front. First, the parliamentary faction, *Rossiiskoe Edinstvo* (Russian Unity), has united "patriots" already in elected office. Upon leaving *Narodnoe Soglasie* (People's Accord), Viktor Aksiuchits and Mikhail Astafiev joined forces with people's deputies Sergei Baburin, Vladimir Isakov, and Nikolai Pavlov to form this new anti-Yeltsin bloc in preparation for the Sixth Congress. Outside of parliament, these deputies organized the *Rossiiskoe Natsional'noe Sobranie* (Russian National Council) in February 1992. Founding-member organizations included the Russian Christian Democratic Movement, the Russian Constitutional Democratic Party (Astafiev), the *Vozrozhdenie* (Revival) Party, the National Republican Party of Russia (Nikolai Lysenko), the Russian National Union, the People's Labor Union, the Russian Merchants' Union, the Union of Russian Cossacks, the International Fund of Slavonic Culture, and representatives from Christian and national

patriotic groups from the Baltics, Ukraine, the Transdniestr
Republic, Gagauzia, the Crimea, South Ossetia, and Kazakhstan.
As declared by the organizers, the *Rossiiskoe Natsional'noe
Sobranie* aims to unite not all patriotic forces, but only those of a
"pragmatic" disposition.[33] Although several leaders of this bloc
are former members of the CPSU, this group tends to be more
"brown" than "red," concerned more with discipline, tradition,
authority, national greatness, and order than with income redistri-
bution or state ownership of the means of production. Most of
these personalities and organizations joined or expressed sympa-
thy for the National Salvation Front. Viktor Aksiuchits was the
notable exception who refused to join, claiming that the Front was
too Communist.

Newly invigorated *Pamyat'* (memory) organizations and the
Liberal Democratic Party, headed by Vladimir Zhirinovsky, constitute a second kind of nationalist organization. These groups
espouse a much more explicitly racist and anti-Semitic rhetoric
than *Rossiiskoe Edinstvo* and its affiliates. Individuals affiliated
with these organizations have never participated in government
or Communist Party structures and tend to advocate extreme, and
often violent, methods for restoring Russia's greatness. Even the
National Salvation Front refused to allow these groups to join its
coalition, asserting that they were too militant.

A third patriotic force to organize since the August coup is the
Rossiiskii Natsional'nii Sobor (Russian National Assembly),
headed by former KGB General Aleksandr Sterligov. In addition to
Sterligov, writer Valentin Rasputin was elected cochair at the orga-
nization's June congress. Other prominent participants in the
June meeting included General Albert Makashov, Vasilii Belov,
Gennadii Zyuganov, Yurii Vlasov, and Aleksandr Nevzorov. The
Assembly has united former military officials, Communists, and
Russian nationalist writers and intellectuals in their rejection of
both communism and democracy and their pursuit of a third,
Slavic way for Russia. The specific content of this special path has
never been clearly articulated, but disenchantment with Western
systems, Communist and capitalist alike, has fueled curiosity in
this organization's appeal for a uniquely Russian course out of the
current crisis. The image of Russia as neither East nor West but
something uniquely in-between has a long tradition in Russian

culture and literature to which leaders of this organization constantly allude. Most of these nationalists joined the National Salvation Front, except General Sterligov himself.

Cossacks constitute a fourth force undergoing a renaissance in post-Communist Russia, with the reorganization of prerevolutionary Cossak detachments throughout southern Russia. Although less overtly racist than figures such as Vladimir Zhirinovsky, these newly formed Cossack organizations advocate more authoritarian measures, including military force, for restoring order and reviving Russia. Several Cossack units even support President Yeltsin.[34]

Finally, successors to the CPSU constitute a fifth flank of this red-brown coalition. Like its democratic counterparts, the Communist movement initially divided into several different parties and movements after the coup. As early as February 1992, however, nine political parties had already claimed to be the successor to the CPSU. Neo-Communist groups to form after the coup include *Trudovaya Moskva* (Working Moscow), *Trudovaya Rossiya* (Working Russia), the Union of Communists, the Working Party of Communists, the Socialist Party of Workers, the Marxist Workers' Party, the "Defense" Independent Trade Union of Workers (*Nezavisimyi Profsoyuz Rabochikh 'Zashita'*), the Russian Communist Workers' Party, *Nashi* (Ours), the Party of Popular Prosperity, the Federation of Communist Movements, the All-Union Communist Party of Bolsheviks, the Worker-Peasant Socialist Party, and a new *Komsomol*.[35] The political orientation of these groups ranges from the almost social democratic orientation of the Socialist Party of Workers, led by Roy Medvedev, to the neo-Stalinist All-Union Communist Party of Bolsheviks, led by Nina Andreeva. Several of these parties united with the nationalists to form the National Salvation Front. As with every other grouping, however, significant figures such as Viktor Anpilov refused to join.

The Constitutional Court's decision to lift the ban on the CPSU in November 1992 ignited a comprehensive campaign to revive a united Russian Communist Party.[36] Beginning in January 1993, local Communist Party conferences were conducted in every region of Russia as a strategy to create the impression of a newly revitalized, grass-roots Communist movement.[37] This process culminated in the Congress of the Communist Party of the Russian Federation, held on February 14–15, 1993 in Moscow.

Six hundred and fifty-one delegates representing more than 500,000 newly registered Communist Party members attended, making the Communist Party of the Russian Federation immediately the largest political party in Russia. Gennadii Zuganov—former secretary of the Central Committee of the Russian Communist Party and current cochair of the National Salvation Front—was elected chairman of the Presidium, further cementing ties between the nationalist and Communist camps.

The economy. The nationalists and the Communists have extremely divergent platforms on economic reform. The Russian Communist Workers' Party, for example, has vehemently rejected privatization and the market in favor of a return to communism. Viktor Aksiuchits, on the other hand, wants his coalition "to represent a classical conservative spectrum of parties similar to Western Christian parties and the Republican Party in the USA."[38] This ideological orientation, of course, includes support for a market economy, but a *Russian* market economy that will "stress the development of Russian business rather than rely on Western capital."[39] In a similar vein, Gennadii Zyuganov has cited the Japanese model to argue that the government must organize and protect local entrepreneurs against Western capital. Sterligov's Russian National Assembly would allow small-scale privatization, but large enterprises and farms must be owned according to Russia's unique collective heritage. There are also extreme conservative groups such as Dmitrii Vasiliev's National Patriotic Front, *Pamyat'*, which reject both communism and capitalism as Western, Masonic, and Jewish, to be avoided at all costs. *Pamyat's* utopia is a Russian agrarian state where everyone returns to the countryside to toil the land.

The state. The broad divisions within the red-brown coalition regarding economic policy are eclipsed by near unity regarding questions of Russian and Soviet state power. From neonationalist to neo-Communist, all these organizations unequivocally support the preservation of the Russian state while the majority long for the revival of the Soviet Union. As Viktor Aksiuchits has proclaimed, "We are convinced that the country's economic revival, cultural blossoming, and political revival are possible only if we halt the collapse of our state and common abode and revive Russian statehood."[40] Going one step further, Vladimir

Zhirinovsky has called for the restoration of Russia's nineteenth-century territorial borders.

As for the cause of the Soviet collapse and Russia's incapacitation, all groups within this bloc blame Yeltsin and his government for acting as lackeys for Western interests. Most infamously, *Den'* (Day) published telegrams allegedly from Secretary of State James Baker to Foreign Minister Andrei Kozyrev with instructions regarding Russian foreign policy. As General Sterligov warned,

> we believe that a threat, a real danger of their destruction, looms over the Russian people. Russia has traditionally prevented the West from having access to enormous stocks of raw material. To get to these stocks Russia must be smashed and its peoples set against each other. For that they must dislodge Russia's pivot—the Russians.[41]

To prevent Russia's colonization, these nationalist-Communist forces have called for the end of military conversion, increases in government spending for the army and the military industrial complex, and a ban on foreign investment.[42]

Tactics. Most of the red-brown groups (with the exception of *Rossiiskoe Edinstvo*) have relied on revolutionary means to mobilize their ranks; the seizure of power is their ultimate objective. (*Rossiiskoe Edinstvo* has advocated parliamentary methods for struggling with the Yeltsin regime.) Beginning with the anniversary of the October Revolution, and especially in response to the creation of the Commonwealth of Independent States, these parties have organized street demonstrations on an almost biweekly basis. Several of these demonstrations, including most notably the February 23, 1992 meeting in recognition of Soviet Army Day, have resulted in violent clashes with the police. Besides general meetings, the red-brown coalition has organized pickets and demonstrations for specific objectives. Their most successful act was a prolonged picket at the Ostankino television station, in which they demanded air time for their views. Russian special forces finally used force to disperse the demonstration, but Yegor Yakovlev, then director of Ostankino, did concede to the nationalist-Communist coalition a weekly television show, "Oppositsiya" (opposition).[43]

Besides public demonstrations, these groups and especially the Communist organizations have courted workers' collectives and trade unions, actively urging them to wage massive strike campaigns. To disseminate their message, the red-brown coalition publishes several newspapers, now much more prevalent at city kiosks than "democratic" publications.[44] The range of tactics does not necessarily stop at demonstrations and rhetoric. Several of these organizations, including most prominently the Cossacks, have organized paramilitary groups. Cossack detachments were deployed in the Transdniestr Republic to defend Russian citizens against Moldovan attack, while armed members of Zhirinovsky's Liberal Democratic Party have been sent to Iraq and Serbia to defend Russian national interests abroad. Some of the more militant organizations, such as the Russian Communist Workers' Party, have warned that a mass armed uprising may be necessary to dislodge the present Russian government.

Prospects. The red-brown coalition is situated on the most precarious coalition of social groups—the over-60-year-old crowd that longs for the stability of the Communist past and alienated and anarchic youth seeking revolutionary confrontation for lack of an identifiable alternative. Whether social support for this coalition will wither or grow depends entirely on the success or failure of Yeltsin's economic reform. In "flat" civil societies such as Russia's that are undergoing acute economic crisis, common denominator ideologies like nationalism can be particularly powerful. That these nondemocratic social organizations still exist, and continue to consolidate through such formations as the National Salvation Front, already threatens democratic consolidation in Russia. In other cases of democratic consolidation, radical movements have been either co-opted into "normal" politics or isolated and eventually defeated in political competition by other means.[45] Russia has not succeeded in either of these two strategies. As Yeltsin himself has warned, "If Russia fails in its reforms, notably economic ones, a dictator will arise."[46]

Conclusion

Political formations in post-Communist nations reflect an emerging, nascent civil society in rapid transition. As such, these political associations are extremely fragile and subject to inevitable change as social groups dissolve and coalesce in response to Russia's new socioeconomic conditions. None of the three major political groupings has a stable social base. As Juan Linz and Alfred Stepan have noted, "In all post-totalitarian polities the relative flatness of the landscape of civil society has created problems for politicians, because it is hard to represent amorphous groups."[47] Most strikingly, Russia's social movements have yet to develop into strong political parties, making organization, aggregation, and articulation of interests difficult for both state bodies and civic actors.

These structural impediments to party formation have been exacerbated by political decisions regarding the timing and nature of elections. *Because Russia has not conducted a post-Communist "founding election" in which political parties controlled candidate lists, contemporary Russian state politics is completely independent of parties.*[48] Unlike the parliaments of East Central Europe, Russian people's deputies were not elected to represent a political program. Without organized parties to monitor and regulate their behavior, Russian parliamentarians simply represent their own individual agendas. Parties and coalitions formed after the 1990 elections have attempted to instill discipline within their parliamentary factions, but with little success.[49] Loyalty to government bureaucracies or individuals is still much more important than the party affiliation. Political leaders already in government do not need parties; parties need them.[50] Without the capability to influence contemporary politics, parties can offer few rewards or incentives for people to join them.[51]

Many Russian party leaders have argued that only elections will "bring parties into the political game" and thereby stabilize the political situation. Without clearly defined social groups represented by stable political parties, however, the menu of outcomes from an election remains highly uncertain. Would fascist leaders be voted into power?[52] Unconstrained by political parties or identifiable social groups, would charismatic leaders mobilize oppositional sentiment to thwart market reforms and rebuff democratic processes? Would anyone bother to vote? In July 1992, a by-election held in Dmitrov for a vacated seat to the Russian parliament attracted only 28 percent of eligible voters.

Most citizens of the Russian Federation have not identified with or become organized into any political organization. Perhaps apathy during difficult times is inevitable, if not even conducive to change. If the majority must suffer decreased standards of living in the short term to make long-term economic reform stick, impassivity at least impedes the mobilization of an antireform opposition against the state. Although a weak civil society will inhibit democratic consolidation over the long run, it may be beneficial for socioeconomic transformation in the near future.

Comparative Conclusions

Until 1989 no country had ever attempted to build a democratic political system while simultaneously creating a market economy. Given the enormity of this task, we should expect the experiments with democracy and capitalism in East Central Europe and Russia to fail.

At least in the short run, revolutions rarely produce democratic outcomes.[1] And radical economic reform, not to speak of overhauling an entire economic system, has often required authoritarian controls, coercion, even violent repression. By this record, what is truly remarkable about the transitions in the former Communist states is not that their new institutions work poorly but that they work at all. This achievement, however tentative, should be seen as an amazing and unexpected consequence of the collapse of communism.

To be sure, the transition has taken different forms in each country. Yeltsin has ruled Russia by decree; Hungarian parliamentary democracy resembles many other Continental polities. Are these simply different paths to democracy, or do they lead to different, even antithetical, results? It is obviously too early to be certain.

Rather than predict the fate of post-Communist democracies, this final chapter summarizes those factors that continue to govern the transitions. This comparison underscores the sharp differences between the countries of East Central Europe and Russia. Although enduring democratic systems in Poland, Hungary, the Czech Republic, and even Slovakia seem likely, the probability of democracy in Russia is much less certain.

The Nature of the Ancien Régime

The more liberal the ancien régime at the beginning of the transition period, the more continuity between old and new during the transition. This hypothesis, derived from transitions in other regions of the world, also holds true for Eastern Europe.[2] Buoyed by a false sense of legitimacy, Hungary's very liberal Communist regime steered the beginning of the transition from above, negotiating elections while ensuring that basic institutional arrangements of the state were left intact. In Poland, the Communist regime had suffered a gradual erosion throughout the 1980s, while the opposition, despite the collapse of Solidarity in 1981, remained widespread and militant. President Jaruzelski tried to "pact" a transition and thereby preserve some old institutions (including his own office). The pact failed, however, when the weaknesses of the ancien régime were exposed. Poland's ancien régime left little scaffolding with which to structure a transition to democratic rule. In Czechoslovakia and the Soviet Union, old institutions and orders were undermined entirely during the revolutionary transition, eventually leading to the collapse of both states.

A related conclusion concerns the socioeconomic context in which transitions begin. *The less comprehensive the economic and social change required to establish a market and private property rights, the more stable the political transition to democratic rule.* At one extreme, Hungary started its transition with a thriving second economy already producing goods and services competitive (or oriented toward being competitive) on Western markets. Thus the social basis to support a democracy had begun to form in Hungary well before the Communist regime fell.

At the other extreme, Russia began its transition from authoritarian rule with a social structure fashioned almost entirely by an autarkic command economy. Unlike Hungary's or even Poland's style of communism, Soviet communism had allowed virtually no economic or social activity outside of party-state control. Moreover, Soviet-style communism was in place in Russia for 70 years, not 40, and enjoyed a level of legitimacy never reached in Eastern Europe. Finally, unlike Czechoslovakia or Poland, Russia has little pre-Communist experience with democracy. Vaclav Havel's references to Czechoslovakia's democratic traditions arm him and his colleagues with a discourse not available to Russian leaders.

The Mode of Transition

The more revolutionary the transition, the greater the challenge of consolidating a democratic polity. Again, Hungary and

Russia are the extremes. Hungary's evolutionary transition has helped to produce a unified state, a stable parliamentary system, and a limited number of political parties, all of which are committed to some form of democracy and capitalism. Without a period of polarizing mobilization against an intransigent Communist regime, Hungary's new political organizations emerged as parties, not as anti-Communist social movements. Because the first government was formed by parties rather than by a revolutionary movement like Solidarity or by a charismatic leader like Yeltsin, it was easier for the Hungarian parliament to maintain its primacy as the leading government institution.

Russia's transition, especially after the spring 1990 elections, became polarized between two factions: "democrats" and "Communists." The existence of a united anti-Communist front, Democratic Russia, with a magnetic leader, discouraged the formation of political parties. The high level of conflict between the Soviet ancien régime and Russia's revolutionary challengers during the transition undermined old institutions but at the same time impeded the development of the new ones necessary for a post-Communist democracy. In the post-Communist era, institutions constructed during the Soviet era still linger on, however, in antithetical opposition to the revolutionary agenda of democracy or capitalism.

Poland and Czechoslovakia fall between the Russian and Hungarian extremes. The Polish transition was both negotiated and polarized. Deals between the Communists and Solidarity created continuity between the new and old. Because this pact was negotiated before the total collapse of communism, however, Poland's eventual post-Communist political forces were still organized as a united anti-Communist movement, effective at opposing a state but ineffective at operating within one.[3] As Adam Przeworski has noted, "social movements are an ambiguous actor under democracy, and always short-lived. Unions have a place to go: industrial relations institutions and the state; parties have parliaments; and lobbies have bureaus; but movements have no institutions to direct themselves to."[4] The process of transforming a social movement (already elected into parliament) into competing political parties after communism had already collapsed exacerbated Poland's problems of democratic consolidation and government stability.

The Czechoslovak transition also was revolutionary, polarized, and sudden. Within weeks, hastily formed social movements assumed full control of the state. No agreement between the old and new ensured the integrity of the state. Civic Forum and Public Against Violence, the two principal revolutionary movements that assumed power, were ethnically based anti-Communist fronts. Had Czechoslovakia's initial political associations been constructed on some other basis, such as class, the split of the Czech lands and Slovakia into two states might have been avoided.[5]

Elections, Timing, and Party Formation

No political factor is more important in the course of democratic consolidation than the timing and sequence of elections. In the post-Communist aftermath, parties move to center stage, often replacing other forms of political associations (movements, united fronts, or trade unions) as the most important nongovernmental political actors. Yet the emergence of vital parties (and a multiparty system) depends on elections, for it is through elections that parties can propagate their ideas, mobilize membership, and acquire a mandate to rule.

Timing is critical: if first elections were held before the collapse of the Communist regimes, the first government has tended to be polarized and unstable. Only elections held after the collapse of the ancien régime allow political parties to form along differentiated social interests. Elections held after the collapse of communism also liberate parliaments and executives from ideological debates about the nature of the existing system.

Hungary was the first country to hold national elections unconstrained by the Communist regime. This timing of elections stimulated party formation while simultaneously eliminating the need for anti-Communist coalitions. Parties became the basic intermediaries between the state and society; parliament, the primary arena of political struggle. Despite a more volatile mode of transition, the timing and sequence of Czech and Slovak elections also promoted party formation and subsequent stable local parliaments at the republic level.

Parties played no part in either of Poland's first two elections, which were referenda first on communism and then on Walesa. Only during the third election did parties have a real role. The election, however, was marked by growing disenchantment with the major parties to emerge from Solidarity, by tremendous party proliferation, and by a poorly designed electoral law, which allowed more than a dozen political parties to take parliamentary seats. This rump parliament created and destroyed three coalition governments in less than a year. A different sequence of elections—in particular, new elections held immediately after the collapse of the Jaruzelski regime—might have produced fewer parties and a more stable parliament.

Even Poland's recurrent government crises, however, do not compare with Russia's electoral and party dilemmas. Russia's first election occurred during a period of intense polarization between "Communist" and "democrat" in which the anti-Communist coalition, Democratic Russia, did not even capture a majority of parliamentary seats. Like Poland's second election, Russia's next experiment with the ballot was a race between Yeltsin and the rest. Parties played virtually no role in either election.

Unlike Eastern Europe, Russia has not held a major post-Communist election. As a result, the deputies in the Russian parliament—still occupied in part by former CPSU members, many of whom ran unopposed during elections when the Communist Party still ruled the Soviet Union—are fiercely divided; fundamental issues have not been decided.[6] The postponement of elections has also stunted the growth of Russia's new political parties, which have yet to compete against one another and thus play little role in post-Communist politics. There was an opportunity to hold elections immediately after the August coup, when "democrats" were heros, Communists were hiding, and nationalists had not yet emerged. Russia's poor sequence of elections has inhibited the stabilization of democratic politics and raised questions about the potential for new elections during the social and economic depression of postcommunism.

Economic Reform and Post-Communist Civil Society

Radical economic transformation has put a heavy strain on these new democracies. Because marketization in Hungary began during Communist rule, that country is less threatened than other East European countries by the stresses of economic reform.

Hungarian associations, social groups, and even parties already have private interests to defend through a democratic polity. To varying degrees, new social groups forged by new market relations and the emergence of private property have also begun to assert their interests in the Czech Republic. Foreign investment, proximity to the West, highly educated work forces, and successful government economic policies have made these two states the wealthiest in the post-Communist world, a development that makes acceptance and viability of the new democratic polities easier there than in other, more economically desperate countries in the region.[7]

In Poland and Slovakia, Communist rule meant the creation of gargantuan, Stalinist-style heavy industry—an economic and social burden that neither Hungary nor the Czech Republic has had to bear.[8] To dismantle these socialist dinosaurs and other legacies of the Soviet economic model, Lech Walesa and other Polish leaders have asked for more authoritarian power. For them, privatization—the key (in their view) to implanting capitalism in Poland—is more important in the short run than the process of democracy. Less enthralled with the wonders of capitalism, Slovakia's new leadership has not—yet—seen the necessity of strengthening the executive authority.

The kind and scope of Russia's requirements for economic transformation dwarf those of Poland, the Czech Republic, Slovakia, and Hungary combined. Bringing 15 million or even 40 million people into a capitalist economy is simply easier than attempting the same with 150 million, especially if they are spread over one-sixth of the earth. Moreover, the depth of state control over the Soviet economy, as already discussed, makes rapid reduction of state power both dangerous and difficult. Finally, those social forces that support such a transformation are still new, weak, and disorganized compared with their counterparts in East Central Europe. Russia's most successful post-Communist political movements have been those based on social groups constructed from past economic arrangements, not newly emerging ones. (Civic Union is the most representative example of this phenomenon.) Because this Russian revolution has been peaceful, these social groups continue to coexist with the newly emerging classes created by the market.

Russian leaders claim to have only two choices: respect democratic processes and allow the old social forces to assume a greater role in government, or empower a (temporary) authoritarian regime capable of smashing the old economic classes. Neither option allows for the simultaneous creation of a democratic polity and a capitalist economy. More than any other factor, the magnitude of this dilemma distinguishes the prospects for consolidation of democracy in Russia from the probabilities of democratic success in East Central Europe.

Territorial Integrity

Questions of territorial integrity have not impeded the institution of democratic polities in either Poland or Hungary. Hungarians living outside of Hungary have mobilized nationalist parties and civic groups, but border revision is not seriously considered. Poland is a true nation-state.

For Czechoslovakia, the issue of defining the state and its borders has eclipsed all others. The options, however, have been clearly defined from the outset: one federal state or two independent states. Ambiguities about imperialism, property rights, and ethnic minority rights have been kept to a minimum. In addition, this issue has been democratically decided. The Czech Republic and Slovakia split peacefully, democratically, and without major violations of human rights.

Russia has not been so lucky. The dissolution of the Soviet Union is still highly contested. Many Russians living in newly independent states want to join Russia, as do threatened non-Russian minorities living on Russia's borders. The territorial integrity of the Russian Federation also is threatened both by separatist movements in places like Chechen-Ingushetiya and Tatarstan and by Russian oblasts seeking greater economic and political independence. The range of possible outcomes has not been as clearly articulated as it was in Czechoslovakia, nor have all parties demonstrated a commitment to a democratic process as a method for resolution.

Consensus

As Juan Linz has written, "Ultimately, democratic legitimacy is based on the belief that for that particular country at that particular historical juncture no other type of regime could assure a more successful pursuit of collective goals."[9] Robert Dahl adds, "Without such a consensus no democratic system would long survive the endless irritations and frustrations of elections and party competitions."[10]

National unity and a commitment to the "public good" are hard to measure, but they do bear on the process of democratic consolidation. Institutions such as the Catholic church and a long history of unifying struggle against communism give Polish society a level of consensus about creating a market economy above and beyond the individual interests of different Polish social groups. The trade union core of Solidarity has espoused general support for shock therapy even though blue-collar workers may be most adversely affected. Encouraged by moral authorities as political leaders, the Czech Republic has demonstrated a similar level of national consensus regarding the necessity of "returning to the West," even if this course means economic hardship in the immediate future.

Russia—and to a lesser extent Slovakia—has not reached a consensus about capitalism or even democracy. Neo-Communist and fascist political organizations in Russia still seek to step beyond the bounds of the polity to obtain their alternative objectives. Equally important, and in sharp contrast to the East European pattern, is the ability of resisters to resist. In Eastern Europe, the renunciation of the Brezhnev Doctrine by Soviet leaders disarmed East European hard-line opponents of democratization. In Russia, except for the handful of coup plotters now in jail, all potential challengers to the consolidation of democracy remain free and able to mobilize substantial resources in their cause. In turn, some liberals in Russia have espoused dictatorship, not democracy, as a means of creating a capitalist system.[11] This basic lack of consensus among contenders for political power seriously undermines the viability of the democratic process in Russia.

Globalization of Democracy

A final factor influencing the fate of East European and post-Soviet democracies is the new international context within which they find themselves. When these transitions began, two systems existed in the world: the capitalist system dominated by North

American and West European democracies and the socialist system controlled by the Soviet Union. Now there is only one international system, and in one way or another all the states discussed in this essay seek to join it.

The homogeneity of the post-cold war international order creates powerful incentives for these new democracies to remain democratic (and capitalistic). Entry into the European Community will depend on the maintenance of a stable democracy.[12] States that violate democratic rights run the risk of international censure. Even international financial institutions such as the International Monetary Fund and the World Bank have introduced notions of "good governance" as a condition of assistance. Moreover, democracy's current hegemonic position vis-à-vis other forms of government offers antidemocratic challengers few alternatives. When the world was divided into two spheres, those seeking to institute authoritarian regimes had the political space to do so. Fearing Communist totalitarianism, the United States and other Western states tolerated authoritarian regimes as long as such regimes remained committed to the "capitalist" side of the global divide. In today's post-Communist global order, tolerance for the creation of authoritarian states—especially in the newly emerging democracies of Eastern Europe—has withered.

The closer a country is to Western Europe and the more integrated it is into the international economy, the greater the influence of these external forces on domestic democratic institutions. Here again, the consolidation of democracy looks more likely in East Central Europe than in Russia. Russia's vast size, extended isolation from the Western world, and legacy as a superpower blunt international leverage in favor of democracy. Russian leaders realize that maintaining at least the veneer of a democracy is a necessary condition for remaining a member of the international community, but the actual content of this democratic polity will be decided by Russians alone. International pressures on Russia to democratize may actually fuel anti-Western sentiment rather than induce compliance.

Democracies after Communism

Poland, Hungary, the Czech Republic, and Slovakia have taken different paths in building democratic systems. In Hungary, the move was evolutionary and controlled; in Poland, negotiated but confrontational; in Czechoslovakia, revolutionary but peaceful. The democratic polities emerging from these different paths have distinctive features and special problems. Hungary has produced a stable multiparty parliamentary system; Poland, an unstable parliament and an independent president; Czechoslovakia, two separate states.

Despite these variations, each of these new polities still meets the basic requirements of a democratic system. Larry Diamond, Juan Linz, and Seymour Martin Lipset have defined democracy as

> a system of government that meets three essential conditions: meaningful and extensive *competition* among individuals and groups (especially political parties) for all effective positions of government power, at regular intervals and excluding the use of force; a highly inclusive level of *political participation* in the selection of leaders and policies, at least through regular and fair elections, such that no major (adult) social group is excluded; and a level of *civil and political liberties*—freedom of expression, freedom of the press, freedom to form and join organizations—sufficient to ensure the integrity of political competition and participation.[13]

All of East Central Europe's new democracies permit competition, encourage political participation, and guarantee basic civil and political liberties. The process of democracy has become increasingly regularized as parliaments learn to function according to standard rules, elections are repeated, and the peaceful transfer of power between governments takes place. According to Laurence Whitehead, an increasing emphasis on the process of decision making rather than the substance of decisions is a good indicator of democratic consolidation.[14] Given the hardships involved in simultaneous transformation of the state and the economy, public enthusiasm for democracy has dramatically dwindled and participation in civic organizations remains low. Yet this disenchantment has not eroded the basic legitimacy of these new democratic polities. None of them has been compelled to use force or coercion to continue economic reform. As noted above, apathy at this stage in the transition may be a blessing in disguise for the long-term prospects of democratic consolidation.

By these criteria, Russia stands apart from Eastern Europe. Although only a year old as an independent state, Russia has not held major elections. Government positions—governors, mayors, and cabinet ministers—are filled by appointment, not election. Without elections, the political participation of most independent political associations, and especially parties, has remained restricted and dormant. Compared to the Soviet regime, most Russian citizens enjoy extensive civil and political liberties. Recent incidents of censorship, suppression of demonstrations, and abuses of the legal process, however, raise doubts about the current regime's real commitment to human rights. Armed conflicts on several of Russia's borders raise the specter that Russia's revolution may not remain peaceful. And, as most dramatically demonstrated during the crisis in government in March 1993, regular democratic processes—the rules of the game for political competition—have hardly begun to take hold; instead, Russia's political actors and institutions either change the rules when unsatisfied with outcomes or move outside of the established boundaries of the polity to realize their objectives. Finally, many of the intervening factors and forces aiding democratic consolidation in East Central Europe are not present in the Russian situation.

This assessment does not mean that Russia's new political system is undemocratic, nor that Russian democracy is certain to fail. Russia has only begun the transition from communism, and the obstacles to building strong democratic institutions there are much greater than in any other post-Communist regime. If Russia succeeds in transforming simultaneously both its political and its economic systems, it will be one of the greatest social revolutions in modern times. If this massive feat of social engineering is accomplished without major civil or international war, it will be the greatest peaceful transformation ever. Measured by these challenges, Russia's new democracy has performed fairly well. Yet continued success is far from certain. The prospects for democracy also looked promising in France in 1790 and in Russia in the spring of 1917. As these examples suggest, nothing is harder than predicting the outcome of a revolution while it is still under way.

Notes

Introduction

1. Sigmund Neumann, "The International Civil War," *World Politics* 1, no. 1 (April 1949): 333–334. The term *revolution* is problematic, laden with normative assumptions. Most scholars of revolutions, including Marxists, political conflicts theorists, and functionalists, subsume this basic description within their definitions of revolution. Disagreements arise when other features, such as class conflict, violence, or individual relative deprivation, are added to the definition. For discussions of the different definitions of revolutions, see Peter Calvert, *Revolutionary and Counter-Revolution* (Minneapolis: University of Minnesota Press, 1990); Chalmers Johnson, *Revolutionary Change* (Stanford: Stanford University Press, 1982); Theda Skocpol, *States and Social Revolutions: A Comparative Analysis of France, Russia, and China* (Cambridge: Cambridge University Press, 1979), chap. 1; Charles Tilly, "Revolutions and Collective Violence," in Fred Greenstein and Nelson Polsby, eds., *Handbook on Political Science* (Reading, Mass.: Addison-Wesley, 1975) 3: 483–555.

2. On the important distinction between revolutionary situations and revolutionary outcomes, see Charles Tilly, *From Mobilization to Revolution* (Reading, Mass.: Addison-Wesley, 1978), 189–200; and Samuel Huntington, *Political Order in Changing Societies* (New Haven: Yale University Press, 1968), 268. Marxist theorists of revolutions, of course, would not accept this kind of contingency. See Skocpol, *States and Social Revolutions* (n. 1, above), 5.

3. For the contrasting cases, see Adam Przeworski, "Problems in the Study of Transition to Democracy," in Guillermo O'Donnell, Philippe Schmitter, and Laurence Whitehead, eds., *Transitions from Authoritarian Rule: Comparative Perspectives* (Baltimore: Johns Hopkins University Press, 1986), vol. 3; Guillermo O'Donnell and Philippe Schmitter, eds., *Transitions from Authoritarian Rule: Tentative Conclusions about Uncertain Democracies* (Baltimore: Johns Hopkins University Press, 1986),

vol. 4; and Terry Karl, "Dilemmas of Democratization in Latin America," *Comparative Politics* 23, no. 1 (October 1990).

4. This relationship creates a paradox for democratic leaders who also seek radical economic transformation because gradualism in economic reform can impede truly revolutionary change altogether. See Anders Åslund, *Post-Communist Economic Revolutions: How Big a Bang?* Significant Issues Series, vol. 14, no. 9 (Washington, D.C.: Center for Strategic and International Studies, 1992).

5. The timing of elections also influences the economic reform process. See ibid., 33.

6. On the importance of founding elections, see O'Donnell and Schmitter, eds., *Transitions from Authoritarian Rule: Tentative Conclusions,* (n. 3, above) 61–64.

7. See Giovanni Sartori, *The Theory of Democracy Revisited. Part One: The Contemporary Debate* (Chatham, N.J.: Chatham House Publishers, 1987), 90–91. Instead of fundamental issues, Sartori used the phrase *ultimate values.*

8. The Communist Party of the Soviet Union (CPSU) was not an electoral party in March 1990. Rather, it was the organizational apparatus that ruled the Soviet state.

9. At the time of this writing, President Yeltsin and the Presidium of the Congress of People's Deputies had just agreed to hold elections for both the presidency and the parliament in fall 1993. The Congress as a whole, however, rejected the idea, making it again unclear when Russia would hold its first post-Communist election.

10. Some nationalist parties in Poland have revived anti-Semitism as a mobilizing tactic. Because the Jewish population is so small, however, questions of autonomous republics or separate states are not on the agenda in Poland. Of all the countries in Eastern Europe and the former Soviet Union, Poland most closely approximates a genuine nation-state.

Chapter 1. Transitions to Democracy in East Central Europe

1. In using the military to govern, General Jaruzelski crushed Solidarity temporarily but destroyed the PUWP permanently because military officers, not Communist apparatchiks, began to

make all political and economic decisions, resulting in a more liberal and less Communist-type regime. See Bruce Porter, *Red Armies in Crisis*, Significant Issues Series, vol. 13, no. 10 (Washington, D.C.: Center for Strategic and International Studies, 1991), 19, and Adam Bromke, *Eastern Europe in the Aftermath of Solidarity* (New York: Columbia University Press, 1985).

2. These figures are cited in Karen Dawisha, *Eastern Europe, Gorbachev and Reform: The Great Challenge* (Cambridge: Cambridge University Press, 1990), 296.

3. Christine Sadowski, "Civil Society in Poland" (Paper prepared for the Conference on Economy, Society, and Democracy, Washington, D.C., May 1992), 6.

4. I. T. Berend, "East-Central Europe: After Communism What?" *Contention* 1, no. 2 (Winter 1992): 97; Janos Kis, "Post-Communist Politics in Hungary," *Journal of Democracy* 2, no. 3 (Summer 1991): 3–5.

5. Elemer Hankiss, "The 'Second Society': Is There an Alternative Model Emerging in Contemporary Hungary?" reprinted in Ferenc Feher and Andrew Arato, eds., *Crisis and Reform in Eastern Europe* (New Brunswick, N.J.: Transaction Publishers, 1991), 303–334.

6. Lazlo Bruzst, "1989: The Negotiated Revolution in Hungary," *Social Research* 57, no. 2 (Summer 1990): 365–387.

7. In Poland, however, this notion of a second society beyond the purview of the state was understood and practiced by many social groups and organizations, whereas in Czechoslovakia only a small part of the intelligentsia took part in this opposition strategy.

8. Andrew Arato, "Social Theory, Civil Society, and the Transformation of Authoritarian Socialism," in Feher and Arato, eds., *Crisis and Reform in Eastern Europe* (n. 5, above), 22.

9. During the years that Solidarity was banned, dozens of smaller organizations established their own identities independent of the collectivist spirit of Solidarity. In 1986, 80 new associations were officially registered; by 1988 more than 500 had registered. See Alexander Smolar, "The Polish Opposition," in Feher and Arato, *Crisis and Reform in Eastern Europe* (n. 5, above), 175–252.

10. Interview with Karol Modzelewski, August 1991, in *Uncaptive Minds* 4, no. 3(17) (Fall 1991): 102.

11. See Bartlomiej Kaminski, "Systemic Underpinnings of the Transition in Poland: The Shadow of the Roundtable Agreement," *Studies in Comparative Communism* 24, no. 2 (June 1991): 174.

12. Judy Batt has labeled this strategy *defensive liberalism.* See her *East Central Europe from Reform to Transformation* (New York: Council on Foreign Relations Press, 1991), 28.

13. In entering into negotiations with the Polish state, the Polish opposition had to abandon the politics of Adam Michnik's "new evolutionism," a strategy for developing "civil society" outside the control of the state, and instead focus on strategies that served to build a new state. As already noted, "Fighting Solidarity" and the Orange Alternative condemned negotiations with the government as a morally reprehensible strategy that would only tarnish the "democrats" and legitimize the Communists.

14. See Michael Roskin, *The Rebirth of East Europe,* (Englewood Cliffs, N.J.: Prentice Hall, 1991), 148–150.

15. On *ruptura* versus *reforma,* see Nancy Bermeo, "Redemocratization and Transition Elections: A Comparison of Spain and Portugal," *Comparative Politics* 19, no. 2 (January 1987): 213–232.

16. Experiences from other transitions suggest that this condition greatly enhances the rapid consolidation of the new democracy. See J. Samuel Valenzuela, "Democratic Consolidation in Post-Transitional Settings: Notion, Process, and Facilitating Conditions," Working Paper no. 150, (South Bend, Ind.: Kellogg Institute, University of Notre Dame, December 1990), 18–22.

17. Maria Csanadi, "The Diary of Decline: A Case-Study of the Disintegration of the Party in One District in Hungary," *Soviet Studies* 43, no. 6 (1991): 1085–1099.

18. Kis, "Post-Communist Politics in Hungary" (n. 4, above), 5.

19. Imre Pozsgay, for instance, played a role in the creation of the Democratic Forum and continued relations with some of its leading members. See Batt, *East Central Europe from Reform to Transformation* (n. 12, above), 35.

20. Renee de Nevers, *The Soviet Union and Eastern Europe: The End of an Era,* Adelphi Papers no. 289 (London: Brassey's for IISS, March 1990), 33.

21. As in the West German system, voters cast two votes, one for a person and one for a party; 176 seats were allotted to those who won individually, 152 were allocated according to party lists based on 19 counties. The remainder of the 386 members of parliament were determined by national party lists. A party needed to accrue at least 4 percent of the vote to acquire a seat in parliament. This system gave the parties the advantage over local figures or national heroes not affiliated with a party. Hungary's complex election law in this regard allowed newly formed, leaderless political parties to play a major role in the formation of Hungary's first post-Communist government. For details, see Akos Rona-Tas, "The Selected and the Elected: The Making of the Free Parliamentary Elite in Hungary," *East European Politics and Societies* 5, no. 3 (Fall 1992), 372; see also Thomas O. Melia, "Hungary," in Eric C. Bjornlund and Larry Garber, eds., *The New Democratic Frontier: A Country by Country Report on Elections in Central and Eastern Europe* (Washington, D.C.: National Democratic Institute for International Affairs, 1992), 40.

22. The Hungarian Democratic Forum won 42.2 percent of the popular vote to gain 164 seats in the parliament. The Forum formed a government with the Independent Smallholders' Party (with 11.4 percent of the popular vote and 44 seats) and the Christian Democratic People's Party (5.4 percent and 21 seats). See Edith Oltay, "The Coalition Government," *Report on Eastern Europe*, November 29, 1991, pp. 14–18.

23. In June 1989, Havel and other dissidents had published a manifesto called "Just a Few Sentences," which called for immediate democratization. This document constituted the basis of the Civic Forum's program.

Chapter 2. Democratic Polities in East Central Europe

1. Barbara Heyns and Ireneusz Bialecki, "Solidarnosc: Reluctant Vanguard or Makeshift Coalition?" *American Political Science Review* 85, no. 2 (June 1991): 351–370. This analysis of the elections shows that rural districts voted for Solidarity in even greater numbers than urban areas, underscoring the anti-Communist rather than pro-Solidarity content of the vote.

2. The full ramifications of these new electoral laws are difficult to calculate. The first-past-the-post system used for Senate

elections gave the leading Liberal Union Party 21 out of 100 senators, as opposed to 62 out of 460 seats in the Sejm. The Senate was still, however, composed of 21 parties and 6 independents. Extremely decentralized voting districts may have been the countervailing force built into the election law that obviated any potential gains from a winner-take-all system. In addition, the complex and convoluted ballot deterred people from voting, a factor that helped small parties and hurt larger parties. See David McQuaid, "The Parliamentary Elections: A Postmortem," *Report on Eastern Europe*, November 8, 1991, pp. 18–19. After their poor showing in the last elections, the Liberal Union has pushed for a new electoral law with higher threshold levels. See Anna Sabbat-Swidlicka, "Poland's Two Camps Specify Terms for Grand Coalition," *Radio Free Europe/Radio Liberty (RFE/RL) Research Report* 1, no. 18 (May 1, 1992): 16.

3. I am not counting the local elections held in May 1990 as a major election. These elections only yielded a 43 percent turnout of the electorate.

4. During revolutionary challenges, the degree of unity among the opposition forces is often commensurate with their level of effectiveness in overthrowing the ancien régime. Paradoxically, however, the greater the unity and effectiveness of the revolutionary movement, the more difficult the process of establishing a multiparty system in the period of postrevolutionary consolidation. Because of Solidarity's history, party formation, based on divisions between senior Solidarity leaders, was viewed initially as a *negative* phenomenon. See Jerzy Szacki, "Polish Democracy: Dreams and Reality," *Social Research* 58, no. 4 (Winter 1991): 718.

5. ROAD was founded after attempts to create an overarching, progovernment political party out of the Solidarity citizens' committees had failed. ROAD leaders claimed that Walesa initiated the split within Solidarity prematurely, forcing positions on economic reform when unanimity was still needed. See, for instance, an interview with ROAD leader Adam Michnik, in *Glos Poranny*, September 27, 1990, pp. 1, 6, in Foreign Broadcast Information Service (hereafter FBIS) East Europe (hereafter EEU), FBIS-EEU-90-203, October 19, 1990, p. 31; and "The Two Faces of Poland," *Economist*, October 27, 1990, p. 51.

6. The Center Alliance initially coalesced as a lobby to promote Lech Walesa as president in place of Jaruzelski. In supporting Walesa, the alliance advocated "acceleration" of political and economic reform and a cleansing of the government of Communists, including, of course, Jaruzelski himself. Walesa, however, was never a member of the Center Alliance and has since had sharp disagreements with Kaczynski, his former chief adviser and a founder of the Center Alliance. During the presidential elections, however, the Center Alliance supported and was identified with Walesa's candidacy while ROAD supported Mazowiecki. See Louisa Vinton, "Solidarity's Rival Offspring: Center Alliance and Democratic Action," *Report on Eastern Europe*, September 21, 1990, pp. 15–25.

7. Timothy Garton Ash, "Eastern Europe: *Après le Déluge, Nous*," *New York Review of Books*, August 16, 1990.

8. Mazowiecki's Liberal Union was affiliated with Poland's first government, headed by Mazowiecki, while the Center Alliance was affiliated with Walesa's tenure as president. This backlash, common in other newly formed democracies, happens because people who have lived under authoritarian rule think that democracy will be a panacea for all past problems. These expectations are compounded in Communist regimes where people also expect their economic situation to improve.

9. Bronislav Geremek, "Civil Society Then and Now," *Journal of Democracy* 3, no. 2 (April 1992): 9.

10. The Democratic Union received 12.3 percent of the popular vote but 13.5 percent of the Sejm seats, in accordance with Poland's complex electoral laws. For a listing of all party percentages, see David McQuaid, "The Parliamentary Elections: A Postmortem" (n. 2, above), 16.

11. After a failed attempt at forming a government by the Democratic Union, four smaller right-of-center parties joined with the Center Alliance to support Jan Olszewski as prime minister. This government fell in June. The next prime minister, Jan Pawlak, resigned in July after failing to forge an effective coalition. A seven-party coalition then named Anna Suchocka as Poland's latest prime minister. Louisa Vinton, "Poland's Government in Crisis: An End in Sight?" *RFE/RL Research Report* 1, no. 30 (July 24, 1992): 15–25.

12. Louisa Vinton, "Five-Party Coalition Gains Strength," *Report on Eastern Europe*, December 6, 1991, pp. 5–12. Many believed that the level of fragmentation within the parliament would enhance Walesa's bid for greater power. See Stephen Engelberg, "Poland Elects a Fragmented Legislature," *New York Times*, October 28, 1991.

13. Dankwart Rustow, "Transitions to Democracy: Toward a Dynamic Model," *Comparative Politics 2*, no. 3 (April 1970): 351. Rustow even argued that such "national unity" was a prerequisite to democracy.

14. This set of conditions is a consolidated version of Dahl's "procedural minimums." See Robert Dahl, *Dilemmas of Pluralist Democracy* (New Haven, Conn.: Yale University Press, 1982), 11. Philippe Schmitter and Terry Karl, "What Democracy Is . . . and Is Not," *Journal of Democracy 2*, no. 3 (Summer 1991): 81–82.

15. In this sense, unlike most other East European countries, Poland had a civil society to resurrect during liberalization. The kind of civil society that emerged, however, is not the same kind of civil society that will develop (or needs to develop) in a post-Communist Poland.

16. Quoted in Arato, "Social Theory, Civil Society, and the Transformation of Authoritarian Socialism" (chap. 1, n. 8), 21.

17. On "principle" versus "instrument," see Laurence Whitehead, "The Consolidation of Fragile Democracies: A Discussion with Illustrations," in Robert Pastor, ed., *Democracy in the Americas: Stopping the Pendulum* (New York: Holmes and Meier, 1989), 79.

18. Adam Michnik, "Nationalism," *Social Research* 58, no. 4 (Winter 1991): 763.

19. In May 1992, the Polish parliament voted to release secret police files about former informants. Walesa has riposted that Poland should avoid a "witch hunt" and has argued that 95 percent of all former Communist Party members must be absolved of their past activities. See "Poles Vote to Release Party Collaborator Files," *New York Times*, May 29, 1992, p. A-5; and Anna Sabbat-Swidlicka, "Poland: Weak Government, Fractious Sejm, Isolated President," *RFE/RL Research Report* 1, no. 15 (April 10, 1992): 5.

20. For instance, the budget deficit was capped at 5 percent of gross domestic product (GDP) as recommended by the

International Monetary Fund (IMF) despite promises to increase government expenditures on this list of services. See Louisa Vinton, "The Polish Government in Search of a Program," *RFE/RL Research Report* 1, no. 13 (March 1992): 8.

21. Interview with Adam Michnik by Janina Paradowska, first published in *Politika*, June 1, 1991. Quoted here from "The Three Cards Game: An Interview with Adam Michnik," *Telos*, no. 89 (Fall 1991): 95.

22. Poland's ideological spectrum, like those of other East European countries, has begun to assume classical Western divisions between left and right. The major difference between West and East European ideological spectrums centers around nationalism and its relation to economic policy. In Poland, the nationalist and Christian-oriented parties such as the Christian National Union support state intervention in social policy. In the West, nationalist, Christian parties usually lobby against state intervention. Some analysts have suggested that a triangle rather than a left-right line best captures this East European difference. Balint Magyar, "Emerging Political Party Structures in Hungary" (December 1991, manuscript).

23. Quoted in "Political Reforms in Eastern Europe," *Moscow News*, no. 41, October 21–30, 1990, p. 12.

24. According to Szelenyi and Szelenyi, the social democratic "political field" has not yet been represented in Hungarian politics. They refer to the social group advocating this ideological orientation—workers and some segments of the professional class—as the Hungarian silent majority. See Ivan Szelenyi and Szonja Szelenyi, "Classes and Parties in Transition in Postcommunism: The Case of Hungary, 1989–1990," in Christian Lemke and Gary Marks, eds., *The Crisis of Socialism in Europe* (Durham: Duke University Press, 1992), 120; and Judith Pataki, "Main Opposition Party Divided," *Report on Eastern Europe*, November 22, 1991, p. 15.

25. Kis, "Post-Communist Politics in Hungary" (chap. 1, n. 4), 5.

26. Melia, "Hungary" (chap. 1, n. 21), 40.

27. Before the 1992 elections, only four parties registered candidates for all three parliaments. Jiri Pehe, "Czechoslovakia: Parties Register for Elections," *RFE/RL Research Report* 1, no. 18 (May 1, 1992): 20.

28. Western investment in Slovakia accounts for only 5 percent of the $800 million total pumped into Czechoslovakia since 1990. See William Schmidt, "Election in Czechoslovakia Will Be a Test of Tensions," *New York Times*, June 3, 1992, sec. A, p. 4.

29. In the summer of 1992, unemployment in Slovakia was 12 percent, compared to 5 percent for the Czech Republic (ibid.). A survey conducted in April 1991 showed that 40 percent of Slovaks believed that economic change was proceeding too fast, compared to 22 percent of Czechs (*Democracy, Economic Reform and Western Assistance in Czechoslovakia, Hungary, and Poland: A Comparative Public Opinion Survey* [Penn & Schoen Associates, April 1991, manuscript], 18–19.) In this context, disputes between Czechs and Slovaks have erupted over arms production, a major sector of the Slovak economy that Havel (a Czech) has sought to close down (see Leslie Colitt, "Arms and the Man in Slovakia," *Financial Times*, January 22, 1991).

30. William Schmidt, "Where Did Czechoslovakia's Democrats Go?" *New York Times*, June 4, 1992, sec. A, p. 5. Twenty-one parties actually participated in the June 1992 election.

31. Interview with Jan Ruml, June 1991, in *Uncaptive Minds* 4, no. 3(17) (Fall 1991): 83; *RFE/RL Research Report* 1, no. 10 (March 6, 1992): 71.

32. *RFE/RL Daily Report*, No. 82, April 30, 1992, p. 6.

33. Quoted from John Lloyd, "Vaclav Klaus, Czechoslovakia's Finance Minister," *Financial Times*, November 19, 1990.

34. The Civic Democratic Party, the Civic Democratic Alliance, the Christian Democratic Party, and the Christian Democratic Union—People's Party formed a coalition government by holding 105 out of the 200 seats in the Czech parliament. See Jan Obrman, "Czechoslovakia's New Governments," *RFE/RL Research Report* 1, no. 29 (July 17, 1992): 4.

35. In February 1992, the Czech parliament amended its election law to allow coalitions of parties to enter the parliament together if they receive 7 percent or more as a coalition. Coalitions of two parties must get 7 percent, three parties 9 percent, and coalitions of four or more 11 percent; the 5 percent minimum for a single party remains unchanged. The law obviously creates incentives for consolidation and coalition among parties. *RFE/RL Research Report* 1, no. 10 (March 6, 1992): 71.

36. "Vienna ORF Television Network," April 1, 1992, in FBIS-EEU-92-064, April 2, 1992, p. 12. The Slovak National Party was one of the first to call for complete independence. Leslie Colitt, "Slovaks Aim for Break with Prague," *Financial Times,* November 2, 1990.

37. "Vienna ORF Television Network," April 1, 1992 (n. 37, above).

38. Jiri Musil, "Czechoslovakia in the Middle of Transition," *Daedalus* 121, no. 2 (Spring 1992): 184.

39. Quoted from Leslie Colitt, "Frustrated Slovaks Think about Divorce," *Financial Times,* November 8, 1990. See also "Bratislava SMENA," October 11, 1990, in FBIS-EEU-90-242, October 16, 1990, p. 32.

40. Jiri Pehe, "The New Slovak Government and Parliament," *RFE/RL Research Report* 1, no. 28 (July 10, 1992): 32.

Chapter 3. Russia's Transition from Communism

1. For a recent reassessment, see William Odom, "Soviet Politics and After: Old and New Concepts," *World Politics* 45, no. 1 (October 1992): 66–98; and George Breslauer, "In Defense of Sovietology," *Post-Soviet Affairs* 8, no. 3 (July-September 1992): 197–238.

2. O'Donnell and Schmitter, *Transitions from Authoritarian Rule: Tentative Conclusions* (intro., n. 3), 9.

3. In the early years of opposition formation, dissidents played a major role in establishing the terms of the conflict between the Soviet state and the Russian democrats. Most important, a coalition of dissidents called the Democratic Union had established the first non-Communist Party in the Soviet Union in May 1988, declaring as its central principles the dismantling of the cult of Leninism and the creation of a multiparty democracy. The diminishing role of dissidents and the Democratic Union in particular is discussed in the following section.

4. Notable exceptions include the late Andrei Sakharov, Sergei Kovalev (chairman of the Human Rights Committee of the Russian Supreme Soviet), and Father Gleb Yakunin (cochair of Democratic Russia. Of the RSFSR People's Deputies elected in 1990, however, 86 percent were Communist Party members. U.S. Commission on Security and Cooperation in Europe, *Report on*

the Congress of People's Deputies Elections in the Russian Republic (Washington, D.C.: March 28, 1990), iii.

5. David Ost, "The Crisis of Liberalism in Poland," *Telos*, no. 89 (Fall 1991): 91. On the effects of this homogenization during revolutionary situations, see John Keane, *Democracy and Civil Society* (London: Verso, 1988), 13.

6. "Deklaratsiya Partii DC" (Declaration of the Democratic Union), May 8, 1988, (mimeo). At the time, the Democratic Union was a union-wide organization. Later, after many of its activists in other republics joined nationalist, republican-based organizations, the group assumed a Russian orientation.

7. Major Democratic Union demonstrations included August 21, 1988 to mark the twentieth anniversary of the Soviet invasion of Czechoslovakia; September 1988, to commemorate the beginning of the Red Terror (on September 5, 1918); December 1988, to celebrate the international day on human rights; April 1989, to protest the T'bilisi massacre. See *Svobodnoe slovo*, No. 34(64), September 23, 1990, p. 1.

8. "Pis'mo dvenadtsati" (Letter of the Twelve), *Voennoe polozhenie—kak c Nim borot'sya?* (Martial law—how to fight it?), (Moscow: DS-Inform, 1991), p. 2.

9. See Vyacheslav Igrunov, "Public Movements: From Protest to Political Self-Consciousness," in Brad Roberts and Nina Belyaeva, eds.,*After Perestroika: Democracy in the Soviet Union*, CSIS Significant Issue Series, vol. 13, no. 5 (Washington: Center for Strategic and International Studies, 1991), 14–31.

10. For a full explication of this ideology, see the interview with Dmitrii Vasiliev in chapter 3 of Michael McFaul and Sergei Markov, *The Troubled Birth of Russian Democracy: Parties, Personalities, and Programs* (Stanford, Calif.: Hoover Institution Press, 1993).

11. The letter is reprinted in English in Alexander Dallin and Gail Lapidus, eds., *The Soviet System in Crisis: A Reader of Western and Soviet Views* (Boulder, Colo.: Westview Press, 1991), 338–346.

12. "Polozhenie o Vsesoyuznom Samodeyatel'nom Obshchestve 'Edinstvo', Vystupayushchem za Leninizm i Kommunisticheskie Idealy" (Statutes of the All-Union Society, *Edinstvo* (Unity), in support of Leninism and Communist ideals),

Moscow, May 19, 1989, reprinted in B. I. Koval', ed., *Rossiya Segodnya. Politicheskii Portretv Dokumentakh, 1985-1991* (Russia Today. Political portrait of the documents, 1985-1991) (Moscow: Mezhdunarodniya Otnosheniya, 1991), 78–81.

13. "Informatsione Soobschenie o Pervom S'ezde OFT," *Shto Delat?*, no.3, August 1989, p. 1.

14. The nomination process to the conference was also a major catalyzing event for independent political association. Campaigns for Yeltsin's inclusion as a delegate were initiated in Sverdlovsk at the giant Uralmash plant, in Moscow by workers' collectives (later consolidated as the "Committee of 19"), and in Kareliya, from which he was eventually elected. (Author's interview with Lev Shemaev, cofounder of the Committee of 19, Moscow, May 1991). In Moscow, students at the Historical Archive Institute initiated the campaign for Yurii Afanasiev's candidacy as a delegate. See Boris Kagarlitsky, *Farewell Perestroika: A Soviet Chronicle* (London: Verso Press, 1990), 3–4.

15. On July 27, 1989, the Moscow Association of Voters was founded by many of the same people who founded the Moscow Popular Front. The same core of people who founded these two organizations later organized the Democratic Russia Movement.

16. "Moskovskoe Ob'edinenie Izbiratelei" (Moscow association of voters) (mimeo, 1989); and Kagarlitsky, *Farewell Perestroika* (n. 15, above), 31–38. Toward the end of 1988, Valerii Skurlatov did found the Russian popular front. This organization, however, had little to do with the popular fronts based at the city level. On the contrary, the Russian Popular Front had closer ties to *Pamyat'* organizations than to the reform-oriented popular fronts in Moscow or Leningrad. Informal political organization proved to be more difficult in more rural areas, however, as the local CPSU apparat continued to repress non-Communist political activities. See Vladimir Brovkin, "Revolution from Below: Informal Political Associations in Russia 1988-1989," *Soviet Studies* 42, no. 2 (April 1990).

17. The dispute over the word *socialism* was half ideological and half tactical. *Obshchina* leader Aleksandr Asaev and *Grazhdanskoe Dostoinstvo* leader Viktor Zolotarev opposed references to socialism for ideological reasons while committed socialists (not Communists) like Boris Kagarlitsky argued for its

inclusion. Pragmatists such as Oleg Rumyantsev from Democratic *Perestroika* supported the inclusion of socialist rhetoric in the front's documents to appease Communist authorities. (Author's interviews with Boris Kagarlitsky, Aleksandr Shubin of *Obshchina*, and Viktor Zolotarev, spring 1991.) See also Igrunov, "Public Movements" (n. 9, above), 22–24.

18. "Khartiya MNF" (Charter of the Moscow Popular Front), *Grazhdanskii Referendum*, no. 1 (Fall 1989): 2.

19. "Koe-Shto ob eksploitatsii" (Something on exploitation), *Grazhdanskii Referendum*, no. 1 (August 1989): 17–18; "Khartiya MNF" (n. 18, above), 2.

20. Campaigns in Leningrad and Kiev were most successful. For a complete analysis of all these election races, see V. A. Kolosova, N. V. Petrova, L. V. Smirnyagina, et al., *Vesna 89* (Spring 89) (Moscow: Progress, 1990).

21. See Sergei Stankevich and Mikhail Schneider, *Rekomendatsii po Taktike Kandidatov Democraticheskogo Bloka i Ikh Kompanii, 1989-90 g.g.* (Tactical recommendations for Democratic Bloc candidates and others, 1989-1990) (Moscow: Informtsentr Moskovskogo Narodnogo Fronta [Information Center of the Moscow People's Front], 1990).

22. See *Put' progressa i sotsial'noi demokratii: Programmie Tezisi SDPR (proekt)* (The way to progress and social democracy: Theses of the Social Democratic Party of Russia, draft) (Sverdlovsk, October 1990). Most West European social democratic parties, in fact, would not recognize the new Russian social democratic party. Instead, they maintained close relations with the CPSU.

23 . See Sergei Mitrofanov, "Chrezvichainaya Sessiya Mossoveta nachalas no tyt zhe i konchilas" (The Extraordinary Session of the Moscow City Council started but ended at once) *Kommersant'*, no. 48, December 10–17, 1990, p. 13.

Also, to a certain extent, the slogan "all power to the soviets (councils)" accurately described the Soviet system of government because each council had legislative, executive, and even judicial powers. Executive power was vested in the presidium or executive committee (*ispolkom*), but its powers were poorly distinguished from the rest of the legislature. For instance, the chairman of the council had little formal executive power but frequently (especially in Moscow and Leningrad) tried to assume the role of a mayor in the city. Moreover, the executive committee answered to both the chairman of the council and the council as a whole, two groups that were often at odds with each other. On these conflicts in Moscow, see the comments by Sergei Stankevich, Gavriil Popov, and Yurii Luzhkov in *Press-Reliz* (Press release), Mossoviet, No. 20, January 10, 1991. To remedy this poor separation of power between the executive and legislative branches of government, the democrats eventually pushed for and succeeded in creating a presidency at the Russian Federation level and mayors at the local level.

24. "The Times Are Getting Tougher," interview with Gavriil Popov, *Moscow News*, No. 42, October 28–November 4, 1990, p. 7. For plans for reform of the soviet system, see Popov's *Shto Delat'* (What is to be done?), (Moscow: Lanit, November 1990), pp. 12–15 and his "Shto Dal'she?" (What is next?) *Isvestiya*, October 3, 1991; Anatolii Sobchak, "Municipal Government Needs More Power," *Moscow News*, no. 43, November 4–11, 1990, p. 6; Ilya Zaslavsky, "V Strane Nenuzhnikh Sovietov" (In a Country of Unnecessary Councils) *Stolitsa*, no. 4 (10), January 1991, p. 3; and "Chevo khochet Il'ya Zaslavskii?" (What does Il'ya Zaslavskii want?) *Moskovskie vedomosti*, no. 2 (14) January 1991, p. 13.

25. On disruptions of food supplies, see *Press-Reliz* (Press release), Mossoviet, no. 10, November 28, 1990; and *Press-Reliz*, Mossoviet, no. 11, November 29, 1990. On the police chief affair, see Boris Pugo, *Reshenie Kollegii Ministerstva Vnutrennikh Del SSSR* (Resolution of the Board of the USSR Ministry of Internal Affairs, MVD), no. Ikm/2, February 4, 1991; "O Bezzakonosti i Proizvole, Chinimom Kollegei MVD SSSR i Generalom Bagdanovom P.S." (Illegality and tyranny, the Obstructive Board of the USSR MVD, and General Bagdanov) (Moscow: Postoyanniya Komissiya po Zakonnosti, Pravoporyadku i Zashchite Prav Grazhdan [Permanent Commission on Legality, Law and Order, and the Protection of Human Rights], February 6, 1991), 3; and Lev Sigal, "Moscow Without Police Chief as Union Blocks City's Liberal Appointment," *Kommersant'*, February 11, 1991, p. 3.

26. Coal miners in the Kuzbass, Donbass, and Vorkuta managed to form political organizations—strike committees and even-

tually the Independent Miners' Union—based on a clearly defined social group. The miners, however, were very suspicious of all political parties. On the role of the miners' strikes in mobilizing opposition to the Soviet regime, see Peter Rutland, "Labor Unrest and Movements in 1989 and 1990," *Soviet Economy* 6, no. 3 (1990): 345–384; L. L. Mal'teva and O. N. Pulyaeva, "What Led to the Strike?" *Soviet Sociology* 30, no. 3 (May–June 1991): 41–48; *Ekspress-Khronika* 10(187), March 5, 1991, p. 1.

27. Oleg Rumyantsev of the Social Democratic Party of Russia, Vladimir Lysenko of the Republican Party of Russia, and Nikolai Travkin of the Democratic Party of Russia regarded Democratic Russia as a coalition of their parties. All of the core organizers of Democratic Russia, however, including Vladimir Bokser, Vera Kriger, Mikhail Schneider, Gavriil Popov, Arkadii Murashev, and Viktor Dmitriev, considered the political parties to be mere appendages of the movement as a whole. Author's interviews and conversations with all of the above in Moscow, January, April, May, June, October, and December 1991.

28. The extent of Gorbachev's complicity in the August coup, however, is still unknown.

Chapter 4. State Building in Post-Communist Russia

1. The fissure of the Czechoslovak state involves the separation of two contiguous nations and not the extraction of an imperial power from its former colonies.

2. See *Ekspress-Kronika*, no. 27(257), July 7, 1992, p. 4.

3. *Analytica: Data Weekly Brief*, no. 12, June 20–27, 1992, p. 4.

4. At present, there exist the Northern Ossetian Autonomous Republic in the Russian Federation and the Southern Ossetian Autonomous Oblast in Georgia.

5. According to Vasily Lipitskii, leader of the People's Party for a Free Russia, 23 Russian regions have now established local trade barriers, while 10 regions have established their own forms of local currency. See the interview with Lipitskii in *Nezavisimaya Gazeta*, July 17, 1992, p. 2.

6. See BBC "Newsnight," March 5, 1992, in *FBIS-Central Eurasia*, FBIS-SOV-92-045, (March 6, 1992), p. 36. *RFE/RL Research Report* 1, no. 9 (February 28, 1992): 84. Aleksandr Bezmenov, "Rossiya nachinaet vikhodit iz sebya (Russia is starting

to exit its own self), *Kommersant'*, no. 24, June 8–15, 1992, p. 19.

7. ITAR-TASS, November 2, 1992, in FBIS-SOV-92-213, November 3, 1992, p. 27.

8. In the days leading up to the election, the Russian Constitutional Court ruled that the referendum was unconstitutional. Several prominent Russian politicians warned that independence would not be tolerated. Finally, on the eve of the election, Yeltsin himself urged the people of Tatarstan to think about the implications of their vote. Although the final wording of the referendum was sufficiently vague to allow for future negotiation with Moscow, 61.4 percent voted for the resolution while only 37.2 percent voted against it—in an autonomous republic where almost 50 percent of the inhabitants are Russian.

9. Since March, some republics, such as Bashkorstan, have gone beyond the terms of the treaty to reaffirm support for the Russian Federation and Yeltsin's government. See the declaration issued by the Bashkorstan parliament as reported in Radik Batirshin, "Malen'kaya republika v 'bol'shoi politike'," (A small republic in big politics) *Nezavisimaya Gazeta*, June 6, 1992, p. 1.

10. In Russian, the prime minister is officially called the chairman of the government.

11. Burbulis was a member of the Interregional Group of Deputies. Besides Yeltsin and Burbulis, the group included such prominent figures as Yurii Afanasiev, Gavriil Popov, Telman Gdlyan, Arkadii Murashev, Andrei Sakharov, Anatolii Sobchak, Sergei Stankevich, and Ilya Zaslavsky. Burbulis also joined Travkin's Democratic Party of Russia for a brief period.

12. For instance, a document called "The *nomenklatura* underground takes charge of the administration of the president of Russia" claims that Yurii Petrov, formerly the Communist Party first secretary in Sverdlovsk, spearheads a clandestine effort that seeks to ensure a political and economic place for the former Soviet *nomenklatura*. The document, however, begins with a disclaimer by the authors that they are unable to prove their allegations. See *Nezavisimaya Gazeta*, January 24, 1992; and Julia Wishnevsky, "Russian Gripped by 'Court Fever'" *RFE/RL Research Report* 1, no. 10 (March 6, 1992): 5; and Vasily Lipitskii, "Revoliutsiya—eto tisyachi novikh vakansii (Revolution means thousands of new vacancies)," *Nezavisimaya Gazeta,* March 27,

1992, p. 2. Lipitskii is executive chairman of the People's Party for a Free Russia (Rutskoi's Party).

13. Gorbachev first created a security council on the Union level, but the organization never assumed real political power. Until the July decree, Yeltsin's security council served a similar, undefined function.

14. Aleksei Kirpichnikov, "Yuryi Skokov: Novyi Samyi Glavnyi," (The right new chief) *Kommersant'*, no. 28, July 6–13, 1992, p. 2.

15. On Skokov, see Peter Pringle, "Gaidar & Co.: The Best and the Brightest," *Moscow Magazine* (June/July 1992): 31.

16. The new appointment, announced on June 14, 1992, coincided with Yeltsin's visit to the United States. See Betsy McKay, "Gaidar is Named Prime Minister," *Moscow Times*, June 16, 1992, p. 1.

17. John Lloyd, "Yeltsin Suffers Setback as Congress Rejects Gaidar," *Financial Times*, December 10, 1992, p. 16.

18. Aksiuchits, the head of the Russian Christian Democratic Movement, and Mikhail Astafiev, the head of the Constitutional Democratic Party—Party of People's Freedom, are former members of Democratic Russia. Baburin is the head of the parliamentary faction *Rossiya*.

19. In June 1992, *Smena* joined *Grazhdanskii Soyuz* (Civic Union), a major coalition in opposition to Democratic Russia. These new political formations are discussed in detail below.

20. Regional leaders have also used the court against the center. Boris Nemtsev, governor of Nizhni Novgorod, threatened to sue the Russian government for failing to deliver cash supplies to his oblast. Moscow eventually responded.

21. Andrea Bonime-Blanc, *Spain's Transition to Democracy*, (Boulder, Colo.: Westview Press, 1987), 12.

22. See Oleg Rumyantsev, as quoted in TASS, March 7, 1992, in *FBIS-Central Eurasia*, FBIS-SOV-92-047, March 10, 1992, p. 26. Rumyantsev's constitutional draft, however, also grants the president the right to dissolve the parliament and call new elections. Oleg Rumyantsev is the executive secretary of the Constitutional Commission of the Congress of People's Deputies; Yeltsin is still the chairman.

23. At the time of this writing, it remained unclear if the April referendum would be held or if new elections for parliament and the president would be convened first.

24. The president's candidate for the post of governor can be vetoed by a two-thirds majority of the oblast council. In most cases, Yeltsin's apparat agreed ahead of time with the local oblast council on a suitable candidate. In some cases, this procedure took months. For instance, because of sharp divisions within the local oblast council, the head of administration for the Saratov oblast was appointed only in March 1992 (author's interview with Saratov oblast deputies, Saratov, August 1992).

25. Darrel Slider, "The CIS: Republican Leaders Confront Local Opposition," *RFE/RL Research Report* 1, no. 10 (March 6, 1992): 8; and author's interviews with local government officials from Rostov, Dubna, Nizhni Novgorod, Tula, Voronezh, Saratov, Ekaterinburg, and St. Petersburg.

26. Author's interviews with officials in the governor's office and people's deputies in the Nizhni Novgorod oblast soviet, (Nizhni Novgorod, August 20–21, 1992). In fact, the local branch of Democratic Russia has split over the issue of whether to support Nemtsov.

27. Anatolii Sobchak, interviewed in *Komsomolskaya Pravda*, March 3, 1992, p. 1, in *FBIS-Central Eurasia*, FBIS-SOV-92-042, March 3, 1992, p. 45.

28. Nikolai Travkin called on Yeltsin to eliminate this dual system of power during his speech at the Sixth Congress of People's Deputies. (*Novosti*, Television News Program, "Ostankino," April 6, 1992).

29. In his resignation statement, Popov once again called for increasing executive power. The statement is reprinted in Tatyana Malkina and Ivan Rodin, "Gavriil Popov ukhodit. Shtobi operedit' Gaidara?" (Gavril Popov quits. To get ahead of Gaidar?), *Nezavisimaya Gazeta*, June 6, 1992, p. 1. Popov claimed to resign because the Russian government would not grant him enough autonomy to carry out the second stage of his economic reforms (author's interview with Sergei Stupar', press secretary for Popov, June 23, 1992).

30. Dmitrii Ol'shanskii, "Vlast' na Otdikhe," (Power over rest) *Rossiya*, no. 32(91), August 5–11, 1992, p. 1.

31. At the Saratov Aviation Plant (SAP), for instance, they have issued "Yermishniki", named after the plant's general director, Aleksandr Yermishin (author's interviews with SAP directors, Saratov, August 22, 1992).

32. *Washington Post*, as cited in Alexander Rahr, "Challenges to Yeltsin's Government," *RFE/RL Research Report* 1, no. 9 (February 28, 1992): 5.

33. In Russia, Igor' Kliamkin and Andranik Migranyan developed this model of the iron hand. See their articles in *Sotsializm i Demokratiya: Diskussionnaya Tribuna (Sbornik Statei)* (Socialism and democracy: A discussion forum [collected articles]), Parts 1 and 2, Moscow: Institut Ekonomiki Mirovoi Sotsialisticheskoi Sistemi) (Institute of Economics of the World's Socialist Systems), 1989–1990.

34. Adam Przeworksi, "The Neoliberal Fallacy," *Journal of Democracy* 3, no. 3 (July 1992): 56.

35. See Robert Dahl, "Why Free Markets Are Not Enough," *Journal of Democracy* 3, no. 3 (July 1992): 85.

Chapter 5. Russia's Post-Communist Political Parties and Social Movements

1. As a coalition of radical dissidents willing to challenge the fundamental tenets of the Soviet regime by means of risky, confrontational tactics, the Democratic Union pushed the terms of the revolution. Once the Democratic Union's agenda became the discourse of mainstream politics, however, the moral purists of the organization refused to participate in "normal" politics. The Democratic Union's demise began when the organization refused to participate in the "Communist-controlled" elections in 1989 and 1990. The roles of dissidents in other former Communist countries also have faded as politics become more normalized. See Michnik, "Nationalism" (chap. 2, n. 18).

2. INTERFAX, February 13, 1992, in FBIS-SOV-92-031, February 14, 1992, p. 44.

3. The Union of Workers' Collectives, which claims to represent more than 3 million workers at large industrial enterprises, is considering joining Civic Union (author's interviews with leaders of the Union, Moscow, July 1992).

4. According to the statutes of the Democratic Russia Movement, the challengers need one-fourth of all regional Democratic Russia organizations and party affiliates to convene such a congress.

5. In the Republican Party, the major split is between Vladimir Lysenko and Vyacheslav Shostakovsky. In the Social Democratic Party of Russia, Oleg Rumyantsev and Boris Orlov have clashed, prompting Rumyantsevto decrease his party activity. In the People's Party for a Free Russia, Grigorii Vodolazov has organized a faction to protest the nationalist statements of his party's leader, Vice President Rutskoi. Oleg Rumyantsev, "Rasstavenie s illyuziya-mi" (Shedding illusions), *Al'ternativa*, no. 24 (October 1992): 1; and author's interviews with Lysenko (October 1992) and Vodolazov (July 1992).

6. After the collapse of the Soviet Union, this coalition split into the International Movement for Democratic Reform and the Russian Movement for Democratic Reform, headed by Gavriil Popov.

7. Igor Kharichev and Viktor Sheinis, "Obrashchenie Sobraniya Grazhdan Rossiiskoi Federatsii k Narodnim Deputatam Rossiiskoi Federatsii" (Address by the Citizens' Assembly of the Russian Federation to the People's Deputies of the Russian Federation), March 26, 1992 (mimeo); and "Obrashchenie Sobraniya Grazhdan Rossiiskoi Federatsii k Vlasti i Narodu" (Address by the Citizens' Assembly of the Russian Federation to the authorities and the people), Moscow, April 5, 1992 (mimeo).

8. In December 1991, the founders of the committees signed an accord with Gennadii Burbulis, then first deputy prime minister of the Russian government, that outlined the terms of cooperation between the civic organization and the government. In agreeing to promote the government economic reforms, the committees gained access to government information, office space, and other facilities.

9. The Committee runs a daily seminar in Moscow about privatization as well as a consulting service in various regional offices. During the first six months of operation, this Committee had given advice to more than 4,000 enterprises. Additionally, the Committee has published a monthly information bulletin called *Zerkalo* (Mirror) and has published *Privatizatsiya: Kommentarii*

v voprosakh i otvetakh, dokumenti i materiali (Privatization: Comments on questions and answers, documents and materials) (Moscow: Respublika, 1992).

10. According to the committees' activists, their conception of privatization formed the basis of the new law (author's interviews with Vera Kriger and Ludmilla Stebenkova, June 26, 1992).

11. "Itogi," Russian television news program, March 28, 1993.

12. Democratic Russia initially criticized Yeltsin for signing the "9 + 1" agreement in April 1991, but not for long.

13. At Democratic Russia's Congress in December 1992, parliamentary leaders Lev Ponomarev and Father Gleb Yakunin were severely criticized for abiding by every Yeltsin decision rather than asserting a political platform of their own.

14. See the interview with Afanasiev in *Det Fri Aktuelt*, in FBIS-SOV-92-026, February 7, 1992, p. 48.

15. The Democratic Platform, formed in January 1990, actually represented the first attempt at a single mass party. After resigning from the CPSU in July 1990, however, Yeltsin refused to join the Democratic Platform in its new incarnation as the Republican Party of Russia (founded in November 1990), stating that 30 years of party service was enough for anyone. See *Demokraticheskaya Platforma*, no.2, April 1990, pp. 1-6.

16. Author's interviews with two *dovernie litsa*, Viktor Dmitriev and Vladimir Lysenko, and two of the co-coordinators of Democratic Russia's presidential election campaign, Mikhail Schneider and Vladimir Bokser (Moscow, June 1991).

17. Leaders of Democratic Russia claim that Gaidar's appointment was the result of their lobbying Yeltsin. Four leaders of Democratic Russia met with President Yeltsin on November 5, 1991, to discuss Russia's new government. At this meeting, Viktor Dmitriev, a Democratic Russia cochair at the time, said, "Boris Nikolaevich, try to understand that if you choose Gaidar, we'll do everything to support his work...but if somebody is nominated from the old government whom we do not trust, then we'll shake Russia until the government resigns, and the sooner the better." (Quoted in Pringle, "Gaidar & Co.: The Best and the Brightest" [chap. 4, n. 15], 31.) The author corroborated this episode with interviews with Viktor Dmitriev (January 1992) and Vladimir Bokser (July 1992).

18. Travkin eventually heeded the advice of his associates within the Democratic Party and refused to join the "red-brown" bloc. Travkin's partners in *Narodnoe Soglasie* (Peoples' Accord), Aksiuchits and Astafiev, eventually did join ranks with these nationalist groups in forming the Congress of Nationalist Forces in February 1992.

19. The Union of Industrialists and Entrepreneurs claims to represent 70 percent of all Russian directors (authors' interview with Aleksandr Vladislavlev, deputy chairman of the union, Moscow, July 1992.)

20. Civic Union leaders conspicuously leave the old CPSU *nomenklatura* off this list because most of their supporters hail from this social group.

21. "Grazhdanskii Soyuz i 'Idyet na Vi'" (Civic Union and 'Go to you'), *Nezavisimaya Gazeta*, July 17, 1992, p. 2.

22. See "Programma Antikrizisnogo Uregulirovaniya" (Program of anticrisis regulation), *Grazhdanskii Soyuz* (Moscow, 1992 mimeographed): 13–23; and "Dvenadstat' Shagov ot Propasti" (Twelve steps from the abyss), *Grazhdanskii Soyuz* (Moscow, undated, mimeographed): 1–8.

23. In declaring Russia's independence in the summer of 1990, Yeltsin used nationalistic sentiment to pit Russia against the Soviet regime. This brand of nationalism, however, aimed to destroy the Union. In his quest to seek allies against the Union, Yeltsin called upon autonomous republics within the Russian Federation to assume as much autonomy as they were able. In this context, those in favor of a strong state (Soviet, Russian, or otherwise) were considered antidemocratic. Since the coup, Yeltsin and his advisers have sought to regain the nationalist mantle. In the spring, his chief adviser at the time, Gennadii Burbulis, made a series of speeches in which he claimed the new economic reforms would lead to the "revival of Russia." (Gennadii Burbulis, TASS, March 22, 1992, in *FBIS: Central Eurasia*, FBIS-SOV-92-056, March 23, 1992, p. 35.) In the summer of 1992, Yeltsin became increasing strident against IMF demands on Russian economic policy.

24. During a trip to Germany in 1991, Travkin came to appreciate the necessity of preserving rights for minority opinions even in majoritarian democratic governments. He was concerned not

so much, however, with minorities living within the Soviet Union as with Russian minorities living in other republics (author's interview with Aleksandr Terekhov, who at the time was a deputy chairman of the Democratic Party of Russia, Moscow, May 1991).

25. Vladimir Lukin, Russia's ambassador to the United States, has labeled this position "enlightened nationalism." See Vladimir Lukin, "Our Security Predicament," *Foreign Policy*, no. 88 (Fall 1992): 57–75.

26. TASS, March 11, 1992; *Rossiiskaya Gazeta*, March 5, 1992, p. 5, in *FBIS-Central Eurasia*, FBIS-SOV-92-049, March 12, 1992, p. 35.

27. During the standoff between the president and the Congress in March 1993, however, both Shumeiko and Chernomyrdin firmly sided with the president, while several Civic Union leaders, including Travkin and Rutskoi, sided with the Congress.

28. In interviews conducted in August, October, and December 1992 with a dozen directors of large (10,000 employees or more) enterprises within the military industrial complex in Moscow, St. Petersburg, Saratov, and Nizhni Novgorod, only one director supported Civic Union. The directors interviewed, however, were selected randomly and do not necessarily reflect the general population of state factory managers.

29. Most significantly, the Committee for Industry and Energy of the Supreme Soviet, the Industrial Union faction, and the Higher Economics Council organized the "All-Russian Meeting of Manufacturers" on August 13, 1992. The meeting included more than 2,000 industrial and agrarian directors as well as people's deputies, bankers, and stock brokers critical of the government. Although Volsky spoke at this meeting, many individual factory directors called for the creation of a new association of industrialists independent of Volsky's organization.

30. In a survey conducted by Popov's Russian Movement for Democratic Reform (RDDR), the democratic party that has been most hostile toward Civic Union, Rutskoi was rated the most popular figure in the country; 53 percent of the 1,202 people interviewed gave Rutskoi a favorable rating compared to 32 percent for Yeltsin. Travkin received a 24 percent favorable rating. ("O resul'tatakh sotsiologicheskogo issledovaniya: RDDR: Otnoshenie Rossiyan k yego initsiativam, tselyam, lideram" [Results of a socio-

logical survey: RDDR: Russia's relations with its initiatives, objectives, and leaders] mimeo, Moscow: RDDR, 1992, p. 1.) These high-profile political figures, however, also may precipitate the destruction of this coalition because Rutskoi, Travkin, and Volsky are unaccustomed to sharing power. The potential for conflict between Rutskoi and Travkin is particularly likely because both are strong-willed, charismatic leaders.

31. According to one Moscow poll conducted by the Institute of Sociology of Parliamentarism, Rutskoi's approval rating moved from 17 percent on February 13, 1992 to 32 percent on June 25, 1992. (See Nugzar Betaneli, "Moskvichei trevozhit blizhaishee budushchee" (Muscovites worry about the near future), *Izvestiya*, June 29, 1992, p. 3. By July, his popularity exceeded Yeltsin's.

32. Edict No. 1308 of the Russian president, "On Measures to Protect the Russian Constitutional System," *Rossiiskaya Gazeta*, October 30, 1992, p. 2, in FBIS-SOV-92-211, October 30, 1992, p. 13.

33. See PostFactum, quoting Mikhail Astafiev, February 27, 1992, in *FBIS-Central Eurasia*, FBIS-SOV-92-042, March 3, 1992, p. 46.

34. "Sokranii Yazik—Sokranii Sebya" (Reducing the language means reducing oneself), *Donskii Voiskoviya Vedomosti*, no. 9(16), 1992, pp. 4–5.

35. See *Rabochii*, no. 1, (December 1991); "Informatsionnoe Soobshchenie" (Information report), *Nasha Rossiya*, no. 20, 1991, p. 2; "Oktyabr'skii Manifest Kommunisticheskikh Dvizhenii" (October Manifesto of the Communist Movement), *Nasha Rossiya*, no. 21, 1991, p. 4; "Uchrezhdena RKRP" (Founding of the RKRP), *Molniya*, no. 28, December 1991, p. 2; United Front of Workers (OFT), *Kontrargumenti i Fakti*, no. 1(10), 1992, p. 3.

36. Anatolii Minaiev, "Soyuz Kommunistov Karelii: Pervyi Shag," *Pravda*, January 10, 1993, p. 2.

37. "Partiinyie Konferentsii v Rossii (Party conference in Russia), *Glasnost'*, no. 6, February 1993, p. 5.

38. Viktor Aksiuchits, INTERFAX, February 13, 1992, in FBIS-SOV-92-031, February 14, 1992, p. 43.

39. Ibid., 44. Before entering politics, Aksiuchits was a successful entrepreneur said to have earned millions during the *perestroika* era.

40. Moscow Teleradiokompaniya Ostankino Television First Program Network, February 28, 1992, in *FBIS-Central Eurasia*, FBIS-SOV-92-042, March 3, 1992, p. 47.

41. *Pravda*, March 3, 1992, pp. 1-2, in *FBIS-Central Eurasia*, FBIS-SOV-92-044, March 5, 1992, p. 55.

42. See, for instance, "Osnovanie Napravleniya Raboti RKRP po Problemam Oboroni i Besopastnosti Strani" (Basic directives of the RKRP work on problems of national defense and security), *Za rabochee delo*, no. 7, July 31, 1992, p. 3.

43. The protestors claimed that several people were killed during this raid. An official investigation, however, found no evidence of casualties.

Neo-Communist leaders considered the *Ostankino* campaign a major victory. See Viktor Anpilov, "Ostankino: Shag k pobede" (A step towards victory), *Molniya*, no. 38, July 1992, p. 1.

44. Only pornography is more readily available. Major nationalist papers include *Den'* (Day), *Otechestvo* (Fatherland), and *Russkoe voskresenie* (Russian revival). Major Communist publications include *Molnya* (Flash), *Nash vybor* (Our choice), *Rabochii* (Worker), *Bor'ba* (Struggle), and *Kontrargumenti i Fakti* (Counterarguments and facts).

45. See the comparison of interwar Germany and France in Seymour Martin Lipset, *The First New Nation* (New York: Basic Books, 1963), chap. 22.

46. *RFE/RL Daily Report*, no. 26, February 7, 1992, p. 1.

47. Juan Linz and Alfred Stepan, "Political Identities and Electoral Sequences: Spain, the Soviet Union, and Yugoslavia," *Daedalus* 121, no. 2 (Spring 1992): 123.

48. See O'Donnell and Schmitter, eds., *Transitions from Authoritarian Rule: Tentative Conclusions* (intro., n. 3), 57–64.

49. A striking example was the inability of Civic Union to deliver its voter bloc during a vote on Yegor Gaidar's candidacy for prime minister during the Seventh Congress of People's Deputies in December 1992. Before the Congress opened, Civic Union cut a deal with President Yeltsin whereby Civic Union would vote for Gaidar in return for the removal of several lesser government officials and the adoption of a compromise economic plan. Civic Union could not deliver even half of its alleged 40 percent of the votes, however, in a secret ballot.

50. Russian law actually establishes disincentives for joining a political party. In seeking to extract the Communist Party from the state, the Russian Congress of People's Deputies passed a law in June 1990 that stipulated that ranking members in a party could not simultaneously hold ministerial posts or chairs on councils or even committees with the RSFSR Supreme Soviet. Although aimed at the CPSU, the decrees also affected several new party leaders including Nikolai Travkin, who resigned as chairman of the RSFSR Supreme Soviet Commission on local government to retain his position as chairman of the Democratic Party of Russia, and Gavriil Popov, who resigned as cochairman of Democratic Russia to maintain his position as chairman of the Moscow City Council. Popov later was again charged with violating this restriction when he became chairman of the Russian Movement for Democratic Reform. See "Popov gotov ostavit' sebe odnu dolzhnost' "(Popov ready to retain one position), *Nezavisimaya Gazeta*, April 1, 1992, p. 1.

51. Taking the long-term view, the Democratic Party of Russia has turned to conducting a business school, with the aim of creating its social base for the next elections. See Aleksandr Kasatov, "Demokraticheskaya Partiya Rossii vzyalas' za delo" (The Democratic Party of Russia gets down to business), *Stolitsa*, no. 23 (81), 1992, p. 5.

52. In December 1991, this was Gavriil Popov's prediction. Many election experts for Democratic Russia also believe this to be a likely outcome of the next elections (author's conversation with Gavriil Popov, December 1991, and interviews with Democratic Russia leaders Vera Kriger, Vladimir Bokser, and Mikhail Schneider, June 1992).

Chapter 6. Comparative Conclusions

1. See Juan Linz, *Crisis, Breakdown, and Reequilibrium* (Baltimore, Md.: The Johns Hopkins University Press, 1978), 13.

2. Valenzuela, "Democratic Consolidation in Post-Transitional Settings" (chap.1, n. 16), 18–22.

3. During the period of forging anti-Communist social movements, groupings were determined not so much by ideological beliefs as by personal relations, the solidarity of opposition politics, or one's relationship with the former Communist rulers. On

Poland, see Garton Ash, "Eastern Europe: *Après le Deluge*, Nous" (chap. 2, n. 7). On Russia, see chapter one of McFaul and Markov, *The Troubled Birth of Russian Democracy* (chap. 2, n. 10).

4. Adam Przeworski, *Democracy and the Market: Political and Economic Reforms in Eastern Europe and Latin America* (Cambridge: Cambridge University Press, 1991), 11, fn. 4.

5. Jiri Musil, for instance, has argued that the crisis could have been avoided if a new constitution had been drafted immediately after the collapse of communism. See Musil, "Czechoslovakia in the Middle of Transition" (chap. 2, n. 39), 184–185.

6. In comparison with parliaments in Eastern Europe, the illegitimacy of this Congress should not be underestimated. In March 1990, more than 80 percent of the elected deputies were CPSU members. At the time, the CPSU still enjoyed tremendous resource advantages over any non-Communist challengers in the campaign, and in many rural regions CPSU leaders ran unopposed. Of course, many CPSU members, including Yeltsin himself, had already advocated democratic reforms. The majority of CPSU participants in this election, however, were loyal CPSU supporters. Moreover, they were second-string CPSU members, as the most prominent party members already had seats in the Soviet Congress of People's Deputies.

7. The correlation between economic development and democracy is widely recognized, even if the reasons for this relationship are still widely disputed. See Seymour Martin Lipset, "Some Social Requisites of Democracy: Economic Development and Political Legitimacy," *American Political Science Review* 53 (1959); Dietrich Rueschemeyer, Evelyne Huber Stephens, and John Stephens, *Capitalist Development and Democracy* (Chicago: University of Chicago Press, 1992); and Larry Diamond, "Economic Development and Democracy Reconsidered," *American Behavioral Scientist* 35, no. 4/5 (March/June 1992): 450–499.

8. Poland's private farms, however, give it an additional advantage that neither Slovakia nor Russia has.

9. Linz, *Crisis, Breakdown, and Reequilibrium* (n. 1, above), 18.

10. Robert Dahl, *A Preface to Democratic Theory* (Chicago: University of Chicago Press, 1956), 132–133. See also Lipset, *The First New Nation* (chap. 5, n. 43), 289.

11. In Russia, the most popular alternative to democracy for achieving capitalism is the "iron hand"—an authoritarian regime that would resemble Pinochet's Chile. For explications, see the articles by Klyamkin and Migranyan (chap. 4, n. 34).

12. Speaking about Hungary's new law on minority rights, Foreign Minister Geza Jeszensky made the following candid remark about the role of international forces affecting domestic decisions: "The Council of Europe has very strict admittance criteria which are also applied to Hungary, so we can build on these criteria; they constitute a model for us." *Budapest Magyar Nemzet*, October 13, 1990, in FBIS-EEU-90-201, October 17, 1990, p. 22.

13. Larry Diamond, Juan Linz, and Seymour Martin Lipset, eds., *Democracy in Developing Countries*, vols. 2, 3, 4 (Boulder, Colo.: Lynne Rienner, 1988–1989). Dahl's eight criteria appear in Robert Dahl, *Polyarchy* (New Haven, Conn.: Yale University Press, 1971), 3. O'Donnell and Schmitter's minimalist definition includes "secret balloting, universal adult suffrage, regular elections, partisan competition, associational recognition and access, and executive accountability"; see O'Donnell and Schmitter, *Transitions from Authoritarian Rule: Tentative Conclusions* (intro., n. 3), 8. On scoring democracies, see Michael Coppedge and Wolfgange Reinecke, "Measuring Polyarchy," *Studies in Comparative International Development* 25, no. 1 (Spring 1990): 51–72; and the annual volumes by Raymond Gastil, ed., *Freedom in the World: Political Rights and Civil Liberties* (New York: Freedom House).

14. See Whitehead, "The Consolidation of Fragile Democracies" (chap. 2, n. 17), 80.

Select Bibliography

Interviews with the following people provided much of the background for this book. Unless cited otherwise in the Notes, these interviews were conducted between June 1992 and February 1993. Many of the people listed below acquiesced to several interviews over the course of this writing. I thank them for their time.

Viktor Aksiuchits, People's Deputy of the Russian Congress of People's Deputies (hereafter referred to as People's Deputy); cochair of the faction Russian Unity; chair, Russian Christian Democratic Movement

Vladimir Akimov, Member of the Central Committee, Federation of Independent Trade Unions of Russia

Viktor Balala, People's Deputy; member of the faction *Smena*

Sergei Baburin, People's Deputy; cochair of the faction Russian Unity

Andrei Bogdanov, Chair, Youth Organization of the Democratic Party of Russia

Vladimir Bokser, Member of the Coordinating Council, Democratic Russia

Yurii Boldyrev, Chief State Inspector, Office of the President

Vyacheslav Bragin, People's Deputy; chair of the Russian State Television "Ostankino"

Aleksandr Braginsky, Minister, Moscow City Government

Leonti Byzov, Chief Sociologist of the Supreme Soviet Committee on Problems of Mass Media

Viktor Dmitriev, Chair of the Organizational Committee for the Russian Bank for Reconstruction and Development; former cochair of Democratic Russia

Petr Fedosov, Chair of the Institute of Politics; member of the Political Council, People's Party for a Free Russia

Vladimir Filin, Co-coordinator of the coalition New Russia

Telman Gdlyan, Co-coordinator of the coalition New Russia

Anatoly Golov, Cochair, Democratic Russia, St. Petersburg; People's Deputy of St. Petersburg City Council

Kirill Ignatiev, Member of the Coordinating Council of Democratic Russia; organizational secretary of Democratic Choice

Vyacheslav Igrunov, Head of Research Department, Ministry of Nationalities

Alexei Kara-Murza, Adviser to the President (Office of Gennadii Burbulis) for Political Affairs

Irina Khakamada, General Secretary of the Party of Economic Freedom

Igor Kharichev, Adviser to the President for Political Parties and Organizations

Valery Khomiakov, Chair, Democratic Party of Russia

Aleksandr Krasnoselsky, former adviser to former Acting Prime Minister Yegor Gaidar

Vera Kriger, Member of the Coordinating Council of Democratic Russia

Pavel Kudyukin, Deputy Minister of Labor; member of the board, Social Democratic Party of Russia

Valentin Kuptsov, Chair of the Organizational Committee, Communist Party of the Russian Federation

Vasily Lipitskii, People's Deputy; cochair, People's Party for a Free Russia

Vladimir Lepyokhin, Chair, Association of Youth Organizations of Russia

Vladimir Lysenko, Deputy Minister for Nationalities; cochair, Republican Party of Russia

Aleksandr Mekhanik, General Secretary, Republican Party of Russia

Vladimir Novikov, People's Deputy; chair of the Council of Factions of the Supreme Soviet

Vladimir Podoprigora, People's Deputy

Sergei Polozkov, People's Deputy; cochair of the Union "Renewal"; member of the faction *Smena*

Lev Ponomarev, People's Deputy; cochair, Democratic Russia

Vladimir Rebrikov, People's Deputy

Ilya Roitman, Deputy Chair, Democratic Party of Russia

Oleg Rumyantsev, People's Deputy; secretary of Constitutional Commission

Nikolai Ryzhkov, former prime minister, USSR

Yurii Satarov, Director, INDEM (Information for Democracy); member of the Presidential Council

Mikhail Schneider, Member of the Coordinating Council of Democratic Russia

Vyacheslav Shostakovsky, Cochair, Republican Party of Russia

Ludmilla Stebenkova, Chair, Democratic Russia Foundation

Vladimir Stolypin, Chair of the Political Council, Democratic Party of Russia

Sergei Stupar', Assistant to Sergei Stankevich, Coordinating Council of the Russian Movement for Democratic Reform

Aleksandr Sungurov, Chair, Democratic Party of Russia, St. Petersburg; People's Deputy of St. Petersburg City Council

Vladimir Tikhonov, Chair, League of Cooperators and Businessmen of Russia

Aleksandr Vladislavlev, Cochair of the Union "Renewal"; deputy chair, Russian Union of Industrialists and Entrepreneurs

Grigorii Vodolazov, Member of the Political Council, People's Party for a Free Russia

Father Gleb Yakunin, People's Deputy; cochair, Democratic Russia

Sergei Yushenkov, People's Deputy; coordinator of the faction Radical Democrats

Georgii Zadonskii, People's Deputy; coordinator of the faction Radical Democrats

Vladimir Zharikhin, Member of the Political Council, People's Party for a Free Russia

Vladimir Zhirinovsky, Chair, Liberal Democratic Party

Alexei Zubin, Member of the Political Council, Party of Economic Freedom

Acherson, Neal. *The Polish August*. Harmondsworth, England: Penguin Books, 1981.

Alekseyeva, Ludmilla. *Soviet Dissent: Contemporary Movements for National, Religious, and Human Rights*. Middletown, Conn.: Wesleyan University Press, 1985.

Bollen, Kenneth, and Robert Jackman. "Economic and

Noneconomic Determinants of Political Democracy in the 1960s." In *Research in Political Sociology*, edited by R. G. Braungard. Greenwich, Conn.: Jai Press, 1985.

Bragin, Vyacheslav. *V 'Belom Dome' za Barrikadami* (Inside the "White House": Beyond the barricades). Tver': Knizhnii Klyb, 1991.

Breslauer, George. "Understanding Gorbachev: Diverse Perspectives." *Soviet Economy* 7, no. 2 (April–June 1991): 110–120.

Brumberg, Abraham, ed. *In Quest for Justice: Protest and Dissent in the Soviet Union Today*. New York: Praeger, 1970.

Bruszt, Lazlo. "1989: The Negotiated Revolution in Hungary." *Social Research* 57, no. 2 (Summer 1990): 367.

Bukovsky, Vladimir. *To Build a Castle: My Life as a Dissenter*. New York: Viking Press, 1978.

Charter of the Party for Economic Reform. Moscow, May 1992 (mimeograph).

Colton, Timothy, and Robert Legvold, eds. *After the Soviet Union: From Empire to Nations*. New York: W. W. Norton, 1992.

Davies, Norman. *God's Playground: A History of Poland*, vol. 2. New York: Columbia University Press, 1982.

Dawisha, Karen. *The Kremlin and the Prague Spring*. Berkeley, Calif.: University of California Press, 1984.

Downs, Anthony. *An Economic Theory of Democracy*. New York: Harper & Row, 1957.

Galasi, Peter, and Gyorgy Sziraczki, eds. *Market and Second Economy in Hungary*. Frankfurt: Campus Verlag, 1985.

Garton Ash, Timothy. *The Uses of Adversity*. London: Granta Books, 1989.

Gati, Charles. *Hungary and the Soviet Bloc*. Durham, N.C.: Duke University Press, 1986.

Glenny, Misha. *The Rebirth of History: Eastern Europe in the Age of Democracy*. London: Penguin Books, 1990.

Golan, Galia. *Reform Rule in Czechoslovakia: The Dubcek Era*. Cambridge: Cambridge University Press, 1973.

Goldstone, Jack. "Theories of Revolution: The Third Generation." *World Politics* 32, no. 3 (April 1980): 425-453.

Gorbachev, Yeltsin: 1500 Politicheskogo Protivostoyaniya (Political oppositions). Moscow: Terra, 1992.

Gross, Jan. "Poland: From Civil Society to Polish Nation." In *Eastern Europe in Revolution*, edited by Ivo Banac. Ithaca, N.Y.: Cornell University Press, 1992.

Havel, Vaclav. *Power and the Powerless*. Armonk, N.Y.: M. E. Sharpe, 1985.

Herbst, Jeffrey. *State Politics in Zimbabwe*. Berkeley, Calif.: University of California Press, 1990.

Hofstadter, Richard. *The Idea of a Party Systems*. Berkeley: University of California Press, 1969.

Hough, George. "Understanding Gorbachev: The Importance of Politics." *Soviet Economy* 7, no. 2 (April-June 1991): 89–109.

Jasiewicz, Krzystof. "From Solidarity to Fragmentation." *Journal of Democracy* 3, no. 2 (April 1992): 55–69.

Karl, Terry. "Imposing Consent? Electoralism vs. Democratization in El Salvador." In *Elections and Democratization in Latin America, 1980-1985*, edited by Paul Drake and Eduardo Silva. San Diego, Calif.: Center for Iberian and Latin American Studies, University of California at San Diego, 1986.

Khasbulatov, R. I. "Reformirovanie reform" (Reforming the reform). Moscow, 1992 (unpublished manuscript).

Kornai, Janos. *The Road to a Free Economy: Shifting from a Socialist System, The Example of Hungary*. New York: W. W. Norton, 1990.

March, James, and Johan Olsen. *Rediscovering Institutions*. New York: Free Press, 1989.

Michnik, Adam. *Letters from Prison and Other Essays*. Berkeley: University of California Press, 1985.

Morrison, John. *Boris Yeltsin: From Bolshevik to Democrat*. New York: Dutton, 1991.

O'Donnell, Guillermo. *Modernization and Bureaucratic Authoritarianism*. Berkeley: University of California Press, 1973.

Offe, Claus. "Capitalism by Democratic Design? Democratic Theory Facing the Triple Transition in East Central Europe." *Social Research* 58, no. 4 (Winter 1991): 876.

Pataki, Judith, and John Schiemann. "Constitutional Court Limits Presidential Powers." *Report on Eastern Europe*, October 19, 1991.

Pribylovskii, Vladimir. *Dictionary of Political Parties and Organizations in Russia.* CSIS Significant Issue Series, vol. 14, no. 7. Washington, D.C.: Center for Strategic and International Studies and PostFactum/Interlegal, 1992.

Prodham, Geoffrey, ed. *Securing Democracy: Political Parties and Democratic Consolidation in Southern Europe.* New York: Routledge, 1990.

Reddaway, Peter, ed. *Uncensored Russia: Protest and Dissent in the Soviet Union.* New York: American Heritage, 1972.

Rossiiskoe Dvizhenie Demokraticheskikh Reform (Russian movement of democratic reform). *Konstitutstiya Rossiiskoi Federatsii (proekt)* (Constitution of the Russian Federation [draft]). Moscow: Novosti, 1992.

Rossiya: Partii, Assotsiatsii, Soyuzi, Klubi (Russia: Parties, associations, unions, clubs). Kniga 5 (vol. 5). Moscow: Rau-Press, 1992.

Rubenstein, Joshua. *Soviet Dissidents: Their Struggle for Human Rights.* Boston: Beacon Press, 1980.

Rutland, Peter. *Business Elites and Russian Economic Policy.* Post-Soviet Business Forum. London: Royal Institute of International Affairs, 1992.

Schmitter, Phillipe. "The Consolidation of Democracy and Representation of Social Groups." *American Behavioral Scientist* 35, nos. 4/5 (March/June 1992): 422–449.

Shestoi S'ezd Narodnikh Deputatov Rossiiskoi Federatsii: Dokumenti, Dokladi, Soobshcheniya (Sixth session of the Russian Congress of People's Deputies: Documents, reports, information). Moscow: Respublika, 1992.

Sokolov, Maksim. "Konstitutsionnie Preniya v VS RF: Prishel Sobchak i Proignoriroval Vsekh" (Constitutional debate at the Supreme Soviet of the Russian Federation: Sobchak came and ignored everyone). *Kommersant'*, no. 13, March 23–30, 1992, p. 18.

Staniszkis, Jadwiga. *The Dynamics of Breakthrough in Eastern Europe.* Berkeley: University of California Press, 1991.

_____. *Poland: Self-limiting Revolution.* Princeton, N.J.: Princeton University Press, 1986.

Starr, Frederick S. "The USSR: A Civil Society." *Foreign Policy* 70 (1989).

Stedman, Stephen. *Peacemaking in Civil War*. Boulder, Colo.: Lynne Rienner Publishers, 1991.

Stone, Lawrence. "Theories of Revolution." *World Politics* 18, no. 2 (January 1966): 159–176.

Tarkowska, Elizabeth, and Jacek Tarkowski. "Social Disintegration in Poland: Civil Society and Amoral Familism?" *Telos*, no. 89 (Fall 1991).

Tarrow, Sidney. "Aiming at a Moving Target." *PS: Political Science and Politics* (March 1991): 12–20

Tismaneanu, Vladimir. *Reinventing Politics: Eastern Europe from Stalin to Havel*. New York: The Free Press, 1992.

Tokes, Rudolf. *Dissent in the USSR*. Baltimore, Md.: Johns Hopkins University Press, 1975.

Tolz, Vera. *The USSR's Emerging Multiparty System*. The Washington Papers no. 148. New York: Praeger/Center for Strategic and International Studies, 1990.

Touraine, Alain. *Solidarity: The Analysis of a Social Movement* Cambridge: Cambridge University Press, 1983.

Ulc, Otto. "The Bumpy Road to Czechoslovakia's Velvet Revolution." *Problems of Communism* 41 (May-June 1992): 21.

Valenzuela, J. Samuel. "Labor Movements in Transitions to Democracy." *Comparative Politics* 21, no. 4 (July 1989): 445–471.

"Vs o Zakonnosti Ukazov Prezidenta" (The Supreme Soviet on the legality of the president's decrees). *Nezavisimaya Gazeta*, June 18, 1992, p. 1.

Weigle, Marcia, and Jim Butterfield. "Civil Society in Reforming Communist Regimes." *Comparative Politics* (October 1992).

Whipple, Tim, ed. *After the Velvet Revolution*. Focus on Issues no. 14. New York: Freedom House, 1991.

White, Stephen, Alex Pravda, and Zvi Gitelman, eds. *Developments in Soviet and Post-Soviet Politics*. Durham, N.C.: Duke University Press, 1992.

Yeltsin, Boris. *Ispoved' na Zadannuiu Temu* (Confession on a given theme). Moscow: Ogonek-Variant, 1990.

Zald, Mayer, and John McCarthy, eds. *Social Movements in an Organizational Society: Collected Essays*. New Brunswick, N.J.: Transaction Press, 1987.

Zaslavsky, Viktor. "Nationalism and Democratic Transition in Postcommunist Societies." *Daedalus* 121, no. 2 (Spring 1992): 97–121.

Zubek, Voytek. "The Threshold of Poland's Transition: 1989 Electoral Campaign as the Last Act of a United Solidarity." *Studies in Comparative Communism* 24, no. 4 (December 1991).